Opposit ... ...
Discourse

BLOOMSBURY CLASSICS IN LINGUISTICS

Multimodal Teaching and Learning, *Gunther Kress,
Carey Jewitt, Jon Ogborn and Charalampos Tsatsarelis*
Opposition in Discourse, *Lesley Jeffries*
Second Language Identities, *David Block*
Worlds of Written Discourse, *Vijay Bhatia*

More titles coming soon!

Opposition in Discourse

The Construction of Oppositional Meaning

LESLEY JEFFRIES

BLOOMSBURY

LONDON • NEW DELHI • NEW YORK • SYDNEY

Bloomsbury Academic

An imprint of Bloomsbury Publishing Plc

50 Bedford Square
London
WC1B 3DP
UK

1385 Broadway
New York
NY 10018
USA

www.bloomsbury.com

Bloomsbury is a registered trade mark of Bloomsbury Publishing Plc

First published 2010 by Continuum International Publishing Group

Paperback edition 2011

Bloomsbury Classics in Linguistics edition first published
in 2014 by Bloomsbury Academic

© Lesley Jeffries 2010, 2014

Lesley Jeffries has asserted her right under the Copyright, Designs and
Patents Act, 1988, to be identified as the Author of this work.

British Library Cataloguing-in-Publication Data
A catalogue record for this book is available from the British Library.

ISBN: PB: 978-1-4725-2838-4
ePDF: 978-1-4725-2339-6
ePub: 978-1-4725-2443-0

Library of Congress Cataloging-in-Publication Data
A catalog record for this book is available from the Library of Congress.

Typeset by Deanta Global Publishing Services, Chennai, India
Printed and bound in India

For Chris, who never let me take myself too seriously.

Contents

Acknowledgements

I am indebted to family, friends and colleagues for their help and support during the writing of this book, not least my partner, Dave, and our children, Sam and Ella, who are not even aware of how long the gestation of these ideas has affected their lives. Of many colleagues at the University of Huddersfield, and in the Poetics and Linguistics Association, who have helped me refine and test these ideas, I would like to thank in particular Dan McIntyre, whose good humoured support is unwavering and Matt Davies, whose PhD thesis has taken some of this material in a new and interesting direction which I am proud to be associated with. My thanks to Dan too, and the in-house editorial team for their help in the latter stages of getting the book published, and their care over detail in particular. All remaining errors and problems of conception are my own. The work for this book would not have been completed either without the support of the University of Huddersfield in the form of sabbatical leave, and the AHRC, which supported this project in a matching period of study leave. I am grateful for both.

1

What are opposites?

1.1 Introduction

This study is a contribution to the body of knowledge about what are popularly called *opposites* and sometimes also labelled *antonyms* or *binaries*. I will refer in general to such pairs of lexemes (and later, also to pairs of phrases or even clauses) as **opposites,** though I will also use a range of more specific terms for different kinds of opposites. The phenomenon of their particular semantic relation will most often be referred to as **opposition.** The main studies of opposition in linguistics have traditionally been in the area of lexicology and semantics, though as we shall see there is a small but growing number of studies investigating opposites in context. My main concern will be with pairs of words whose oppositional relationship arises *specifically* from their textual surroundings, which I am naming **constructed opposites, created opposites** or **unconventional opposites** interchangeably, but which have also been variously called **non-systemic semantic opposition** (Mettinger 1994:74), and **non-canonical antonyms** (Murphy 2003:11 and Davies 2008:80). This book will introduce and explore the phenomenon of the textually constructed opposite relation, initially formally and functionally, and then by a series of case studies which will consider its implications for ideological and aesthetic meaning in texts and their contexts of production and reception.[1]

It is important to recognize at the outset that this study relies to some extent on the acceptance of some kind of lexical semantics which hypothesizes that in addition to the cognitive storage of items (lexemes) and rules for their combination (morphology and syntax), human beings also have certain kinds of knowledge about the meaning (sense) relations between these lexical items. Thus, one of the things that we may know about the word *hot* in English is that it is opposite to the word *cold,* and more extreme in relation to temperature than the words *cool* and *warm.* There have been many developments in linguistics since de Saussure made explicit his ideas on the internal structure of human languages, and many of them have challenged the fundamental distinction between **langue** and **parole,** later adapted by Chomsky as a cognitive distinction between **competence** and **performance.** Nevertheless, one of the conclusions of this book will be that in order to explain the cognitive aspects of opposition-creation in texts, we will need to refer to at least some kind of core concept of oppositeness and its realization in lexical relations. This context-free notion of the capacity of words (lexemes) to be related by oppositeness will be referred to below as 'conventional' opposition, to reflect the idea that although there is nothing intrinsic about these relationships, and their importance may vary between languages and cultures, there is nevertheless some kind of tacit agreement between members of speech communities that certain words are formally opposite to each other. This is reflected, of course, in the importance that opposites are accorded in our culture in early education as evidence by the plethora of early books aimed at teaching pre-literate toddlers the core opposites.

I was first alerted to the contextual creation of opposition by an election slogan of the Conservative Party in the 1983 British election. There was a picture of a black man[2] with a slogan underneath reading as follows:

Labour says he's black. Tories say he's British.

The parallel structure of the two clauses in this slogan (*X says Y is Z*) together with the conventional opposition between *Labour* and *Conservative* in Subject position (*X*) and identical content in the opening of the subordinate clause (*he's*) sets up the expectation of a balancing pair of opposites as the two subordinate Complements (*Y*). What we have as a result is *black* and *British* being constructed as a pair of opposites by the advert. The implication is apparently that if the Labour Party calls a man *black,* they are denying his *Britishness.* This is therefore a complementary opposition; it is implied that you cannot be both black and British. This opposition appears to confirm the Conservative Party as one that is non-racist, since they are presented as 'colour blind' and those voters who are looking for that message may thus see them as emphasizing the inclusiveness of their definition of *British.* But the very creation of the complementary opposition *black-British* in itself indicates a potential to see these qualities as incompatible (you can't be British if you do identify yourself as black) – and therefore feeds the prejudices of the racist potential voters too. Here is one (black British) reader's response to this slogan:

> In case I was in any doubt as to what this new black Briton looked like, in 1983 the Conservative party produced an advertisement that featured a photograph of a smartly suited, briefcase-wielding, well-groomed black man under the heading 'Labour says he's black, Tories say he's British.' Unsurprisingly, this black Briton neither looked like me, nor, in fact, did he look like anybody I knew. The Conservative party was soon forced to withdraw this advertisement, after it was pointed out that the terms 'black' and 'British' were not, in fact, mutually exclusive. However, at least we non-white Britons had been afforded a glimpse of one of 'their' images of 'us'. (Phillips 2004)

Caryl Phillips naturally assumes that the Tory advertisement indicates that *black* and *British* are opposites, though the intention may not have been this in fact, and the Conservative Party might use the defence that this is not explicit in the text itself. In fact, the creation of opposites in such contexts is an example of what Grice (1975) calls a **conventional implicature** and Simpson (1993:127–8) calls **pragmatic presupposition.** This, they claim, is the creation of a presupposition or implicature not through the context-free text, but through the text in combination with its context of use. The juxtaposition of two words such as *black* and *British* in parallel structures of this kind and with conventional opposites in the Subject position of each of the parallel structures predisposes the reader to see the words as a pair of opposites. The actual interpretation of this text will depend on the reader, and Caryl Phillips as a black man on the left of the political spectrum naturally assumed that it was the Conservative Party who were racist in proposing this opposition, although their intention was to persuade readers that the Labour Party are more prejudiced because of their insistence on referring to people's skin colour. However, the advertisement was presumably not aimed at those who would *never* vote Conservative, such as Phillips, but rather at those on the left of Conservative supporters who might have been looking for reassurance that the Conservative Party at the time (1983) was minimally not racist (i.e. was colour blind) and also conversely those on the right who were looking for reassurance that the Conservatives were indeed illiberal in their immigration policies (i.e. those who *would* accept that black and British are opposites).

Although presuppositions, even pragmatic ones, might be quite difficult to deny, it is always possible, with some effort, to 'defease' them (see Simpson 1993:134–8) and it is easier with pragmatic than with semantic presuppositions. Defeasing usually takes the form of denial and re-wording of the offending utterance. Here, then, this defeasing might take the form of the Conservative Party saying that they were simply trying to point out that they were more inclusive than Labour, since they accepted all kinds (colours) of people in the category 'British', without the need to point up the differences within that category. Indeed, even an interpretation of oppositeness really ends up indicating that it is Labour who are creating this opposition (i.e. if you're black, you're not British). This audacious implicature turned the accepted wisdom of the time (that it was the Tories who were racist and Labour who were not) on its head, and it was probably for that reason that the advertisement caused such a stir. It was also too subtle for a poster campaign, and as we see in Phillip's passage, is often wrongly interpreted as the Conservatives' *own* attempt at excluding black people from Britishness.

Although this was a fascinating one-off example, I was interested to see whether similar contextually created opposites occurred more widely and in other kinds of text. I therefore began to explore a text type as different as possible from news reporting; namely contemporary poetry. Since contemporary poetry is superficially very different in many ways from advertising slogans or political rhetoric, this was also a way of estimating the extent of this phenomenon in English texts more generally. I very quickly found examples in a number of poems I already knew quite well and in styles as different as Philip Larkin and E. E. Cummings. For example, Larkin builds one of his early love poems (from *The North Ship* 1945) on a number of opposites. Here is the first stanza:

> Is it for now or for always
> The world hangs on a stalk?
> Is it a trick or a trysting place
> The woods we have found to walk?

I have explored this poem in more detail elsewhere (Jeffries 1993:95), but it will serve here as a contrast to the political poster analysed above to illustrate how similar structural/semantic features of text are used by very different texts and with different effects. Stylistics is sometimes accused of 'reading off' meanings from structural and semantic features of texts, most famously in Fish (1981:75), but Simpson (1993:113) argues against this charge of interpretative positivism that there is no automatic assumption about the meaning of a textual feature and he demonstrates this by the use of the same analysis of two stylistically comparable examples to create two rather different interpretative effects. In the case of constructed opposites, the mechanism for creating the opposition may be the same, but the contextual meaning is different. In his poem Larkin sets up our expectations of opposition by using apparently straightforward opposites *now* and *always*, linked by the conjunction *or*, in the first line. We are then led by the recurrent parallel structure *Is it ___ or ___?* to set up further sets of new oppositions in line with the conventional one:

trick	vs.	trysting place
mirage	vs.	miracle
sham	vs.	sign

These oppositions are not conventional in the sense defined above, but their construction as opposites in this context is made more prominent by the alliteration between each pair as well as the shared semantic features of the paradigms with *trick, mirage* and *sham* on the one hand sharing features of deception and unreality whereas *trysting place, miracle* and *sign* on the other hand share semantic features of reality and yet a reality that seems incredible. So, incorporated into this semantic scaffolding, we have Larkin's initial view of love: it is either just a temporary aberration (*now*) with no basis in reality or it is real and everlasting but wonderful (*always*). At the end of the poem Larkin then plays a trick on the reader when he turns the whole structure on its head, acknowledging that the original opposition on which the meaning appeared to be built is faulty, since *now* and *always* are not in fact opposed at all:

> I take you for now and for always,
> For always is always now.

The reader may thus (re-) discover along with Larkin that in addition to *always,* another, rather different opposite of *now* is *never,* while *always* may be seen as simply a series of moments like now (*always now*). The whole anxiety about whether a new love is going to last is therefore shown to be misplaced.

What appeared to be common about these two rather disparate examples from politics and poetry respectively was that they drew on the reader's understanding about some kind of relatively stable semantic relationship between lexemes in English (i.e. opposition) and yet they were contextually creating a similar, though not conventional, opposite between other lexemes with a result that is meaningful in that particular context.

The main aims of this book are to establish some of the parameters of the phenomenon I am calling constructed opposition, using a series of case studies as the focus for answering a number of research questions as follows:

- What is the extent of created opposition across text-types?

- What are the triggers for unconventional opposites?

- What is the relevance to unconventional opposition, if any, of the semantic sub-divisions of antonymy?

- What is the function or meaning of created opposition in particular contexts?

- What insights can we obtain into the process of interpreting unconventional opposition?

Before I discuss a range of detailed examples from the data I have been analysing for created opposition, I will try to frame this study within the context of an understanding of opposition more generally. Some of these sections are inevitably short and cannot do justice to the wealth of thought and research on this topic, but I hope that it will give a sense of how this study may fit into the wider picture.

1.2　Opposition: A history of ideas

This book is about language, and about the contextual use of language in particular. However, it is clear that the notion of two words being opposed to each other semantically in the way that is implied by the term 'opposite' or 'antonym' seems to have a special status in human thought and history. Clearly, many of the most important historical events – usually wars – and most of the world's great religions are based on some kind of conceptual binary.

This section will not be able to trace the whole history of the significance of opposites in human thought and civilization (that is another book) but it will contextualize to some extent the remainder of this study, by demonstrating that there are interesting links between the study of language usage and both psychology and philosophy in relation to concepts of opposition.

Before embarking upon the investigation of linguistic opposition-construction, it is worth pausing to reflect that opposition has been significant to philosophers since pre-Socratic times and has continued to exercise the minds of cultural thinkers since, including Plato (see Cooper and Hutchinson 1997) and Aristotle (see Ackrill 1975), followed by Hegel (1874) as well as in recent years theorists such as Derrida (1967). The nature of the human body (two eyes, ears, legs, arms etc.) has often been claimed to be the source of some of the human ideas of beauty (e.g. Plato and Aristotle) since they claimed that beauty was predicated on some principles including symmetry, which presumes the base two. One might further argue that as well as beauty, other ideas of order (and disorder) may be binary in their most fundamental manifestations. Plato's discussion of opposites in relation to his 'eternal forms' confirms that for him opposites preexist our ability to perceive them, though not all forms have an opposite; thus the property of bed-ness is not opposed by a property of not-bed-ness. Aristotle, by contrast, thought that opposite qualities, such as height, were the result of experience, and that we perceived different heights first and categorized them as opposite (taller-shorter) on the basis of such perceived differences.

It is clear in any case that the existence of opposites has underpinned much of early Greek philosophy, including thinkers before Plato and Aristotle, and informed the development of certain aspects of logic and rhetoric as Lloyd (1966) points out:

> And if Aristotle explicitly investigated the logic of the use of opposites, he also threw some light on the psychology of certain argumentative devices based on opposites which are similar to those we find used in earlier Greek writers. Indeed we saw that in the context of 'rhetorical' arguments he expressly recommends the juxtaposition of contraries as a means of securing admissions from an unwary opponent. (170)

I will return to this persuasive use of opposites in a later chapter, but here I want to note the essential nature of opposites which was tacitly assumed in this period, and saw early Greek thinkers basing much of their work on opposites:

> A large number of theories and explanations which were put forward in early Greek speculative thought may be said to belong to one or other of two simple logical types: the characteristic of the first type is that objects are classified or explained by being related to one or other of a pair of opposite principles. (Lloyd 1966:7)

Though Plato developed ideas about when opposite terms may be applied to subjects, he did not distinguish between the different logical properties of some opposite pairs. Aristotle, by contrast, did make such distinctions, as well as discussing the contextual effect and power of opposite pairs. In discussing the examples of created opposition I found in my data, one of the questions that frequently occurs is whether there is a default type of opposite, the mutually exclusive and exhaustive type ('complementaries' in linguistics) which is assumed in the absence of active information to the contrary. We will return to this question in Chapter Five. There was a tendency in early Greek thought, including Plato's work, to assume that this kind of opposite was indeed the fundamental type. It may be worth pointing out here that so fundamental were the opposites assumed to be that the question of their number and identity is not clearly addressed in a focused way by philosophers of this period; presumably they are thought to be self-evident.

One of the questions that this book will not be able to settle is to what extent (if at all) the phenomenon of opposition is an important structuring principle in human psychology. In other words, I will not be addressing in any detail here the cognitive reality (or otherwise) of the idea of opposites, though some effect will be hypothesized from textual opposition to world-view in later chapters. This is not to say that this is not an interesting question, or an important one. In Psychology there appears to be a willingness to accept these concepts of antonymy and opposition as givens (premises) as illustrated by the assumption in the title of Davern and Cummings (2006), *'Is life dissatisfaction the opposite of life satisfaction?'*, or as incidental, and given, concepts in investigations of other cognitive attributes (e.g. Scott *et al.* 1980 and Estes and Ward 2002). There has also been some work on this question by Murphy and Andrew (1993), who claim that opposition is a conceptual rather than a linguistic phenomenon. Brewer and Brandon Stone (1975) investigate the acquisition of certain antonymic pairs relating to the spatial dimensions and Heidenheimer (1978) studies the emergence of the general category of antonymy in children's language acquisition. Jones and Murphy (2005) also investigated the use of antonyms by children and compared their usage with adults' usage in their child-oriented language. They concluded that children used antonyms more than the adults speaking to them and they suggest that:

Developmental Psychologists have found that children appreciate antonymy from very young ages and grasp the notion without difficulty. (Jones and Murphy 2005:402)

The assumption of the Greek philosophers and implications of psycholinguistic research may both point to the suggestion that opposites are in some sense fundamental to human thought, but there remains relatively little empirical evidence of the cognitive nature of this phenomenon.

However, there has been some *theoretical* speculation on the existence and significance of opposition in human cognition and society and in the absence of hard evidence, this is a good indication that opposition is at least important to human thinking. Following the philosophy of Hegel (1874), Levi-Strauss (1963) and Derrida (1967) in particular have focused on the importance of binary opposition in structuring human perceptions. Hegel is credited with the 'thesis-antithesis-resolution' triad which underlies much of scientific endeavour, though there is some dispute about whether he is indeed the originator of this model. Levi-Strauss, as an anthropologist, observed that human societies were often based on binary divisions, though usually with some kind of equivalence within this division similar in some ways to the resolution of the scientific model. In *Structural Anthropology* (1963), he argues that it is the fundamental properties of the human mind that influence social and cultural structures, and that these are universal. He also suggests that the human mind desires to find a midpoint between the opposites. This is something that it might be useful to revisit in the light of the findings of the study reported in Chapters Two to Four, and particularly in relation to the importance of opposites for conflict situations and their resolution.

Levi-Strauss's ideas influenced Derrida, another significant commentator on cultural structures, but one who rejected the structuralist view of human perceptions and introduced 'decons-truction' as a way of demonstrating the relativity of oppositions, and their effective lack of universality. By contrast with Levi-Strauss, Derrida (1967) claims that though binaries are ubiquitous in human societies, they usually privilege the powerful and there is always inequity between the two terms of culturally and socially significant opposites. His deconstruction programme is aimed at overturning these power structures in favour of the oppressed or powerless party. Needless to say, various oppressed groups in society took up Derrida's ideas to try and find a way to take some power away from the oppressors. Derrida's notion of 'play' in particular was employed by feminist theorists to describe the activities that they undertook as a way of deconstructing patriarchal dominance of the gender binary (see, for example, Feder *et al.* 1997). I will show later that many of the constructed opposites in my data seem to have some kind of preferred or more powerful term and are contrasted with a less attractive or less powerful term, even when they are completely unconventional as opposites.

Note that, like Plato and Aristotle before them, most of the theorists mentioned above are interested more in the mutually exclusive/ exhaustive binary than the other categories, such as gradable or converse types of opposite. This is never explicitly because of their power or their frequency of occurrence, though one might speculate that these are the reasons why such opposites get more attention than the other categories. The Hegelian notion of the resolution of binaries is also left hanging with very little comment in later work.

The emphasis on opposites in the history of human thought, then, ranges from the assumption that they are in some sense 'given' to the notion that they are constructed by social norms. Whether there is some conjunction of these two positions in reality is not often questioned, though it seems perfectly reasonable to presume that human beings may be pre-programmed to structure their experience of the world in a binary manner, without presuming that any *particular* aspect of the world is so-determined. As for discussion of socially constructed opposites, such as gender, how such constructions come about is often ascribed to textual representation in its broadest sense (e.g. Cranny-Francis 2003 see below), though the mechanisms for how this may occur linguistically or semiotically are frequently left implicit. Where the process of division is considered, the linguistic aspects are usually taken for granted:

> this idea of sex, of a natural biological coupling and equivalence, is part and parcel of the establishment in certain Western cultures of a battle of the sexes, of a binary opposition, which makes this

distinction and mutual exclusiveness between men and women appear natural. (Cranny-Francis *et al.* 2003:4)

This example demonstrates that the debate is usually sociological and political and almost never linguistic, as a later extract from the same source shows:

How do we know? Administrative forms ask us to tick male or female, doors to public toilets make us choose one or the other, the birth of a new baby is invariably greeted with the question. 'Boy or girl?' (Cranny-Francis *et al.* 2003:5)

In summary, one might suggest that although the existence of opposites has been taken for granted for many thousands of years, and although they are apparently common in all languages in the world, there is still a long way to go before we can argue that they are indeed a deep-seated structuring device of human cognition. However, we can look at socio-cultural as well as linguistic evidence in favour of the hypothesis that opposition is a very important structuring device in our (at least Western) society and that it may well, for that reason, have some echo in our cognitive make-up, whether that is of our very nature or whether it is nurtured by the contexts in which we live.

1.3 Opposition in logic and maths

The Traditional Square of Opposition (see Figure 1.1 below) originated from Aristotle and has been the subject of a great deal of debate since. It aims to represent the logical relationships between the four basic kinds of proposition (universal negative, universal positive, particular negative and particular positive) in graphical form and is interesting for my purposes here because it demonstrates the fact that oppositional meaning differs when you talk about the meaning of individual linguistic items (usually words) and when you consider sentences or the propositions that underlie them. In the square of opposition, the concern is with what are known as the 'universal propositions'

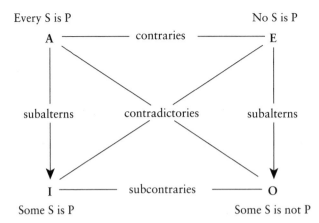

Every S is P   No S is P

A ———————— contraries ———————— E

subalterns   contradictories   subalterns

I ————————— subcontraries ————————— O

Some S is P   Some S is not P

FIGURE 1.1 *The Square of Opposition. (http://plato.stanford.edu/entries/ square/)*

and the relationship is therefore between statements of truth about categories of things or people, rather than the decontextual meanings of individual words. The square of opposition perhaps demonstrates more than anything the lack of fit between what we know about the way that language works and the logic that arises from debates in philosophy. While some of the logical properties of opposition may be interesting to us when we as speakers of English notice them, they are for the most part beneath the radar of everyday linguistic usage.

Another logical principle, the 'principle of excluded middle' is a logical law discussed by Aristotle (Ackrill 1975), Peirce (1931–35, 1958) and many others and referring to the truth values of propositions again, rather than items (such as words) themselves. The law states that 'everything must be or not be' and that there is no middle way between these extremes. While this may be logically the case, and many of our commonest uses of opposites assume this to be the case, by being treated as complementaries, it is also true that in real life there are many areas where we may want to argue that something both is and is not. This is particularly true of gradable properties, such as adjectival meanings, where one might argue that the property of tallness, for example, both is and isn't present in a person who is reasonably, but not stunningly, tall. We will look at the logical properties that are of some interest in relation to opposites in the next section.

1.4 Opposition in language

Though linguists have taken note of much of the theoretical debate in philosophy and cultural studies about the importance and nature of opposition, they have themselves contributed a great deal of detailed understanding to the study of linguistic opposition. Sapir (1944), Lyons (1977) and Cruse (1986, 2004) are among those who moved the debate on in thinking through the possible semantic models which would fit what we know about opposites in language. Sapir, for example, pointed out a cognitive feature of opposites which I will return to, and which underlies the construction of unconventional opposites as much as the use of conventional pairs of opposites:

> To the naïve, every person is either good or bad; if he cannot be easily placed, he is rather part good and part bad than just humanly normal or neither good nor bad (Sapir 1944:101, quoted in Lyons 1977:277)

This tendency to presume complementarity when faced with any opposite has already been noted and will form an important part of the discussion in later chapters. Lyons makes much the same point in his assessment of 'what appears to be the human tendency to categorize experience in terms of dichotomous contrasts' (1977:277).

Another important observation made by Lyons relates to the common directional opposites that he observes. These support his explanation of Plato's shortcomings in failing to differentiate between gradable and non-gradable contrary properties, with the result that he struggled to reconcile the fact that objects can seem to have two contradictory qualities like 'tallness' and 'shortness' at the same time.

It would be difficult to exaggerate the importance of directional opposition, both deictic and non-deictic, as a structural relation.

It is all-pervasive in both the grammatical and the lexical structure of languages; it is central to the analysis of the grammatical categories in tense, aspect and case and the personal and demonstrative pronouns, and it is the basis of much that we might think of as metaphorical in the use of particular lexemes and expressions. Furthermore, it may well be that our understanding, not only of directional opposition, but of opposition in general, is based upon some kind of analogical extension of distinctions which we first learn to apply with respect to our own orientation and the location or locomotion of other objects in the external world. (1977:281–2)

Note that what Lyons appears to be arguing here is that there is a strong physiological reason behind our ease of acquisition and use of opposites, and that this is carried over from our bodily experience into our conceptualizing of the world. This is not far from Platonic ideas of beauty being based similarly in our appreciation of the symmetrical body, and though it is not proven, it does at least provide an explanation for the apparent ease with which children assimilate such ideas.

To go beyond the physiological explanation of opposites, we may ask more generally to what extent the linguistic division of the world into opposites is genuinely reflective of the world in some direct way. It is probably worth establishing here that language does provide some compelling evidence for the view that many opposites are neither absolute nor 'given', but are reflections of one particular way of viewing the world and the human experience. This is not to argue that there are *no* natural opposites, since that would be to deny the evidence from the natural sciences that, for example, temperature can run in two directions (*hot* and *cold*) and dimensions also objectively have different 'poles' (*big* and *small*, *long* and *short* etc). However, it remains clear from the way in which we use oppositional lexemes that we are able to alter our view of even the apparently most absolute opposites (like *alive-dead*) in a number of ways, and that this may have more to do with personal or political convenience than with physical reality. Thus, to take idiomatic examples, we may use expressions like *half-dead* to exaggerate our exhaustion, or *totally married* to emphasize a couple's commitment to each other (or boring habits). In each case, the 'reality' as constructed in our society is that you cannot be in a state that is half way between being dead and alive, and that despite some problem cases, such as Persistent Vegetative State Syndrome, we generally treat being alive as anything more than being dead. In other words, they are mutually exclusive options. This may not be the way that death is perceived in all societies, however, and it is possible to imagine death as a simple shortcoming of the bodily functions as the novelist Sebastian Faulks imagines in describing a primitive view of death through one of his characters:

> One of the things that has been drawn to my attention is the way that kings, pharaohs and so on were so often buried upright. I had assumed it was because the people did not understand that death was a termination. They thought it was just the breakdown of whatever faculty had proved fatal. So they continued to feed the dead king or god. (Faulks 2006:452)

Although death and life may seem to us like a clear pair of absolute opposites, this is largely as a result of the way that we relate these terms in our language. Thus, we may presume that the weaker version of the Whorfian hypothesis precisely captures this tendency for us to use our language as the structuring device for our outlook on life (and death), though we are clearly also able to think beyond the automatic categorization that is inherent in our language when necessary. Indeed in some cases our idiomatic expressions demonstrate this kind of mental escapology quite clearly.

As in so many cases, then, the language we speak is a reflection, but not a perfect reflection, of what we can perceive about the world through other means, such as science, logic, maths and philosophy. One of the interesting aspects of opposites in language is that the popular view[3] is that they are all the 'same' on some level, though in fact the logical properties of different sub-types of opposites mean that they are really rather different from each other. Cruse (1986:197) argues that 'the overall class is not a well-defined one' despite the fact that 'Of all the relations of sense that semanticists propose, that of oppositeness is probably the most readily apprehended by ordinary speakers.' He also points out that:

> Within the somewhat indeterminate general class of opposites there is a small number of relatively well-defined sub-types (concerning which the intuitions of ordinary speakers are paradoxically uncertain) with interesting and systematic properties. (Cruse 1986:198)

There is a potential project for psychological investigation evident here, to confirm what appears to be the case; that until it is pointed out that they have different logical properties, speakers tend to see all linguistic opposites as being in the same category. The reality of this categorization for speakers may be one of the reasons why all opposites tend to converge on the complementary (mutually exclusive) type in speakers' imaginations.

It is also possible that speakers have a 'folk semantic'[4] view that opposites are words which have utterly different meanings, when only a few moments' thought are enough to realize that far from being utterly different, they are in fact near synonyms whose one different semantic feature has a cultural or social meaning which is significant for that society. I am assuming a particular theory of semantics here that sees word meanings as made up of components that are shared with other words in differing combinations (see Nida 1975). Other ways of describing lexical meaning would be equally suited to the point being made here, which would not alter; words stigmatized as opposites in a language are usually close in meaning, by whatever means this proximity is measured. So, we choose to make 'opposites' out of *good* and *bad*, but we do not normally enhance the one small difference in manner of perambulation between *walking* and *running* into an 'opposite'. Note, however, that children to some extent do try to extend the notion of opposites to all words and this is why adults have a residual memory of seeing *cats* and *dogs* as opposites at a period in their lives when these constituted the whole of the animal kingdom, or even *walk* and *run*, though they often apologize for being 'silly'[5] if they bring these up as examples.

Cruse (1986) also focuses on this point, observing that the similarities between the terms of an opposite pair extend to their distributional properties, which are often identical, and the tendency to substitute some terms for their opposite in error. This, it seems to me, is particularly true of those pairs labelled converses (see below), where we get *lend* and *borrow* being confused (*Can I lend your pen for a moment?*) for example. Cruse also points out the fact that:

> Philosophers and others from Heraclitus to Jung have noted the tendency of things to slip into their opposite states; and many have remarked on the thin dividing line between love and hate, genius and madness, etc. The paradox of simultaneous difference and similarity is partly resolved by the fact that opposites typically differ along only one dimension of meaning: in respect of all other features they are identical, hence their semantic closeness; along the dimension of difference, they occupy opposing poles, hence the feeling of difference. (Cruse 1986:197)

I will suggest later that this property of opposites – their semantic closeness and ability to 'flip' between poles is significant for the development of future human affairs. For now I wish to investigate the different categorizations of opposite that have been put forward.

The finer possible categories that Cruse (1986) points out are based on his assessment of the way in which conventional opposites are regularly used in conversation. This semantic 'snapshot' of the range of use of certain lexemes contributes to our understanding of the point at which the langue and parole meet; the repetitious uses that build up into a pattern of usage which looks very much like a code. However, as with many semantic patterns, it is relatively easy to find counter-examples for these usage patterns of opposites, and the subtler points of Cruse's observations then appear to be less embedded in speaker consciousness, and thus less available to the speaker as a basis on which to interpret the created opposites with which I am concerned here.

Nevertheless, there is some evidence in the data explored in this book that the main sub-categories of opposites regularly identified by linguists and lexicologists do sometimes impinge on the creation and interpretation of textually constructed opposite pairs. We will therefore deal with these four categories here.

1.4.1 *Mutual exclusivity*

I am using the logical properties of these sub-categories of opposition as the headings for the sub-sections because there is a proliferation of terminology in this area, and the reader may have different experience of these terms, particularly where the history of ideas is concerned, as philosophers have used a different set of labels for a similar set of ideas. The mutually exclusive type of opposite is often known as complementary in the linguistic tradition, though it also characterizes what is usually meant by binaries in cultural theory and possibly also the distinction between privatives and positives of Aristotle. The important issue for us here is that it is in a way the stereotypical opposite in that it admits no intervening values between its extremes and thus reflects the principle of the excluded middle. In addition to this mutual exclusivity, we might include among the vital attributes of this most typical of opposites the idea of exhaustiveness, since we could envisage two mutually exclusive terms which might nevertheless not cover between them the whole of the relevant semantic field and thus not be seen as opposites. For example, the pair *animate-inanimate* are normally seen as dividing the range of possibilities of concrete items in the world into two, there being nothing known which is either half way between *animate* and *inanimate* nor anything that exists outside this particular division. Note that it is only the concrete world that is divided by these terms; the abstract world does not normally require description in such terms. The logical property of complementaries as a result of these characteristics, is that in denying one term we assert the other. Thus, to say that *Jet is a woman* is to effectively deny that *Jet is a man* and vice versa.

This kind of opposite, then, requires the conceptual field that is being characterized (e.g. gender in humans) to be divisible into two parts, and only two parts. Note, incidentally, that the term *complementary* is sometimes used to describe sets of terms more than two in number if they have this same property of covering a whole field of meaning between them. The colour words in any particular language would be one example of this. To return to the dual-complementaries, we may note that such a socially entrenched conceptual division as gender is not affected by the historical existence of hermaphrodites; transsexuals or any other challenges to the distinction between being a woman and a man. Unfortunately for those people who feel that the category ill-fits their identity, as far as the practice of using English is concerned, this is a mutually exclusive categorization. Note again, however, that it is important that such terms are used appropriately for this mutual exclusivity to be relevant. Though it would be possible to imagine saying *This pebble is not alive,* the opposite (*This pebble is dead*) is not a relevant statement here, as the lack of animacy of the pebble makes the dead-alive opposition inapplicable, except in metaphorical usage.

It is also worth noting that the mutually exclusive category of opposite is not a stable and well-defined category, even in relation to conventional linguistic opposites. Thus, although it is clear that we normally treat the *easy-difficult* dimension as gradable (see below), there are occasions when the same opposition will be more likely to be interpreted as mutually exclusive, such as when a bald negative is used. Thus the utterance *this homework is not easy* would most likely be interpreted as *this homework is difficult* unless it were followed by an additional comment such as *but it's not that difficult either.* Note that Cruse calls such examples 'gradable complementaries', though this simply fudges his categories and makes it harder to justify them as categories at all. A better way to deal with the range of possible uses of even individual opposites is to draw on prototype theory (see Rosch 1993, 1998) and hypothesize prototypical examples, such as 'pure' complementaries and 'pure' gradable antonyms. Semanticists would then be able to plot the range of usage of individual cases against these reference points. For my purposes, the contextualized instance is the only reference point, as the examples I am concerned with are mostly unconventional, and one cannot therefore readily appeal to their 'other' instantiations as opposites (though a corpus study may be able to establish how often such pairings are made).

We will return to the question of mutual exclusivity later in relation to textually constructed opposites. Their ubiquity in news reporting and political rhetoric makes them particularly significant in constructing the public's view of the world.

1.4.2 *Mutual dependence*

Although they are perhaps not the second-most stereotypical opposite, the mutually dependent type of opposite, otherwise known as *converses,* is very significant in considering different ways of constructing our view of the world. These opposites include *borrow-lend, husband-wife* and *above-below* and demonstrate that opposition can provide a double perspective on a single set of facts or events. Thus, when a person is lending, someone must be borrowing; for there to be a husband, there must be a wife; if your photo is above the side-table, the side-table must be below your photo.

For Cruse (1986), converses are one type of 'directional' opposite, though he also uses the term 'relational opposite' to include them. He suggests that the most prototypical cases (the paradigm cases) are the spatial ones, usually expressed in prepositional pairs such as *above* and *below,* but he also acknowledges that this relation is found in other kinds of lexical pairings such as *ancestor-descendant* and *master-servant* or *teacher-pupil.* Note that converses are generally thought of as being consistently relevant to each other, even where one is used alone. Thus, 'Jack is a brilliant parent' presupposes that Jack has some children, and 'The doctor made her ward rounds early' presupposes that the doctor has some patients. However, some individual terms in these relationships may on occasion represent a non-converse version of the meaning. Thus *doctor* may be applied to someone with no patients (e.g. a newly qualified or retired doctor) and *child* applies even when the parents are dead. Note that our concern in this book with examples in context means that such general semantic distinctions are of less concern than the particular relation that appears to be holding the example under scrutiny. In many cases it is not possible to distinguish between the different types of opposite where textually constructed examples are concerned.

One of the consequences of the fluidity of boundaries between different categories of opposite, and the lack of awareness on the part of speakers of these distinctions, is that some conventional or established opposites may be challenged and/or have their category changed by a particular contextual use. This presents opportunities for those who wish to challenge the *status quo* as well as those who might wish to manipulate others for their own ends. For example, whether some of the opposites that divide the world in the early twenty-first century by being seen as mutually exclusive might be more productively viewed as mutually dependent is a large question, but it is one that I will return to in the final chapter of this book.

1.4.3 *Gradability*

More clearly central as a category of opposites, the gradable antonyms are by far the most common of the conventional opposites in English, including such text-book favourites as *hot-cold, long-short* and *good-bad.* These opposites are in neither a mutually exclusive nor a mutually dependent relationship as described above, though as we have seen, the same pair of opposites (e.g. *easy-difficult*) can be treated contextually as either gradable or mutually exclusive:

> This concerto is easier than the one I played yesterday. (gradable)
> The concerto is not difficult. (probably interpreted as easy; complementary)

It is also true to say that conventional opposites that are normally treated as mutually exclusive may, in context, be made gradable:

> I feel more alive than I have ever done before!

And some pairs of lexemes have polysemous senses which are complementary in one sense, and gradable in another:

> This prisoner is dead. (complementary: opposite *alive*)
> This battery is almost dead. (gradable: opposite *charged?*)

The relationship between conventional uses and categories of opposite and their use in contexts where these uses and categories can change is an under-researched topic, and it underpins the work reported in this book, which looks at similar processes of adapting conventions in context, but in relation to unconventionally opposed items. We will therefore return to the boundaries between categories of opposition, if indeed they are categories at all, in a later section.

1.4.4 *Reversability*

The final category of opposite that we will consider here is the reversive or directional opposite in which one of the terms of the opposition reverses the process or the direction of the other. These categories are separated out by Cruse (1986) but I will treat them together here as they seem to share some semantic properties. This category includes conventional opposites such as *button* and *unbutton* and directional prepositions such as *up* and *down* (in their dynamic sense). Most of these pairs of opposites can also be used in a static sense, and in this case they are logically more like complementaries or converses than directional or reversive opposites. Compare, for example:

> The bus went up the High Street and then came back down. (directional)
> If tails is up, heads is down. (converses)
> If interest rates are up, they can't at the same time be down. (complementaries)

The conclusion that one might draw from such flexibility is that these so-called logical categories of opposite, while they have theoretical distinctiveness, are often blurred in usage. This might explain the apparently popular conception that these are all the same kind of thing; that opposition is a single relationship. We will return to these categories in the analysis in later chapters, though for now I wish to give a fuller introduction to the kind of contextually created opposite that is at the heart of this investigation.

1.5 Contextual features of opposition

The observations made so far, that the idea of oppositeness is not only ubiquitous but also deep-seated, supports the case for postulating the existence of some kind of relatively stable code or langue which, while not inviolable, is nevertheless stable enough to form the background to the many deviations from that norm that occur on a daily basis. Indeed, it could be argued that without such a construct, we are hard-pressed to explain how readers/hearers are able to decode language on an everyday basis. Specifically, for my purpose here, without at least a psychological understanding of the concept of oppositeness, and probably the language to describe it, we would struggle to interpret created or unconventional opposites. A similar point is made by Shen (2002:212) in the introduction to her article on verbal creativity:

> this theory attempts to account for certain regularities exhibited by figurative language in poetic discourse by suggesting that these regularities reflect a 'compromise' between, on the one hand, aesthetic goals of creativity and novelty and, on the other, a conformity to cognitive constraints that ensure its communicability.

This point could be made appropriately in relation to many of the features of language whereby there is both a regular pattern of usage and some more or less significant departures from this patterning. In the present case, it would mean that speakers may well depend on what they know about conventional opposition to interpret new examples that they encounter.

In this chapter, I have tried to explain and illustrate some of the ways in which textual structures, both syntactic and semantic, can create one-off, temporary opposites which serve the purpose of the text's meaning and yet which rely on the reader's understanding of conventional opposition to decode them. A more thorough account of the different triggers of unconventional opposites and their relationship to conventional opposites will be undertaken in Chapter Two. Here, then, I will simply provide a more detailed account of the phenomenon under scrutiny.

While many of the examples explored here will depend to some extent on the semantic knowledge of speakers, and many have some direct dependence on conventional opposites, there is also a very important syntactic element to the creation of opposites. The syntactic 'frames' we will investigate below are, I would argue, recognized as potential opposite-creating frames by speakers of English. This view is partly supported by corpus-testing of such frames (as for example in Davies 2008) and can be hypothesized as a kind of 'semantic prosody' as explored by Louw (1993), though his investigations so far attach to lexical items rather than structures.

Although other scholars (e.g. Mettinger 1994 and Jones 2002) have considered the syntactic frames in which opposites tend to occur, these studies have so far been focused on the conventional opposites and their use in context. The rare mention of the kind of example I am concerned with here includes a recognition from Mettinger that what he calls 'non-systemic' opposites are yet to be studied in detail:

> It might be noted that non-systemic semantic opposition has not attracted the attention of many structural semanticists. It would, however, be a profitable field of research for any kind of conceptual approach towards the study of meaning-relations. (Mettinger 1994:74)

Apart from this direct recognition of the category that concerns me here, there are only occasional references in research on opposites to unconventional pairings. The following from a study of children's use of opposites discusses the data sentence *Milk is good for you but gum is bad for you*:

> Young children also use antonyms to explain and create oppositions between inanimate items . . . For instance, the contrast set up between *milk* and *gum* is hardly a textbook opposition, but the child has used the basic, known opposition between *good* and *bad* (for you) to understand the relative merit of these items with respect to dental health, and so has created an understanding of *milk* and *gum* that makes them each other's opposite in this context. (Jones and Murphy 2003:376)

Though this is something of a diversion from Jones and Murphy's main theme, it is as good an explanation as I have found of the constructed opposite. It is not clear whether they consider it to be a childhood phenomenon alone, but their description would certainly fit all the examples that I have found.

1.6 Structure of the book

In Chapter Two I attempt to answer the research question 'What are the triggers for unconventional opposites?' and consider their local effect in the context. While the mechanics of how opposites may be created textually are interesting, it is still more interesting, perhaps, to see how these might create particular meanings and at times deliver particular ideologies in their context. Chapter Three, therefore, considers some examples from literary data of such meaningful effects of opposition-construction and Chapter Four introduces case studies of non-literary types of text. These two chapters between them, then, address the following research questions:

- What is the extent of created opposition across text-types?

- What is the relevance to unconventional opposition, if any, of the semantic sub-divisions of antonymy?

- What is the function or meaning of created opposition in particular contexts?

Chapters Three and Four each consist of a series of case studies which explore the nature of the unconventional opposite as exploited in the data under consideration. The larger context of these case studies enables us to see the extent to which constructed opposites may sometimes structure the discourse meaning for a whole text or series of texts.

The final chapter, Chapter Five, returns to the more general task of weighing up the evidence from the earlier chapters and attempting to answer the final research question:

- What insights can we obtain into the process of interpreting unconventional opposition?

In addressing this question, Chapter Five considers the potential that cognitive theories of reading and meaning may have on the data under scrutiny here.

Opposites are, I would claim, one of the most important of the linguistic-cognitive structures by which we categorize and organize our world, and thus also our world-view. One part of the evidence for the conventional nature of many opposites is found in children's books. At a fairly young age, children in English-speaking societies are introduced to opposites, usually via picture books or early books with barely more than one sentence on a page. Where there *is* some syntactic structure, it is usually a pair of parallel structures and they always highlight the opposing words. The first conclusion we can draw from this explicit teaching of opposites is that they are clearly conventional, rather than absolute relationships, if they need to be taught so explicitly. But perhaps a more interesting aspect of this introduction of young people to opposites is that although most of the opposites taught to children are the gradable kind (*hot-cold, tall-short* etc.), the emphasis from the adults teaching them is on the extremes, as though they were *really* complementaries. It is only later, when the important lesson of oppositeness has been learned, that children discover that *hot* and *cold* are connected through a range of intermediate temperatures and their terminology (*warm, cool, tepid* etc.), and that *tall* and *short* are only relative terms. By this time, the 'norm' for opposites, that is that the stereotypical opposite is a complementary, has been established in the young person's world-view.[6] As we shall see in later chapters, this notion of the stereotypical opposite as a complementary is deeply entrenched in many aspects of Western society and it has very serious repercussions for us all. If mutual exclusivity, for example, is the basis of foreign policy in the world's major powers, it may be difficult to envisage ways of reconciling serious differences between them.

2

How opposites are constructed in texts and what they mean

2.1 Introduction

This chapter examines the structural and semantic features of the phenomenon I am calling constructed opposition and considers the common denominator in their meaning potential. While, as we will see in later chapters, there are also *con*textual (i.e. pragmatic) issues that need investigation, for example into the mechanisms for interpreting these unconventional opposites, we first need to establish the extent to which created oppositions are triggered by textual features; the different manifestations of this phenomenon and the basis of their meaning-making.

The findings in this chapter, though applicable more widely, originated in three separate research projects which focused on opposition-creation in different text-types. The first investigated two collections of poetry, Carol Ann Duffy's *Selected Poems* (1994) and Mebdh McGuckian's *Venus and the Rain* (1984, 1994). At the time, I was investigating different stylistic aspects of women's poetry (see, for example, Jeffries 1994) and since these two collections were superficially rather different from each other stylistically, they seemed worth comparing. Chapter Three gives a fuller account of the findings of this project in relation to constructed opposition. The second project which I will draw upon in this chapter was concerned with the reporting of the general election in the last few days before Labour won power in 1997. There is a fuller description of this project in Chapter Four, but some of the examples from this data are used here to support the distinctions being made and to demonstrate that the mechanisms for producing unconventional opposites are the same in different genres, though the interpretations and effects may differ. The final project which I draw upon here is one where I looked at the openings of one hundred novels to see to what extent constructed opposites are present in the initial setting up of a text world. This project is also reported in some detail in Chapter Three, but a small number of examples are used here to broaden the range of genres being used to inform the discussion.

Subsequent to these research projects, the completion of my student, Matt Davies', PhD thesis on this subject in 2008 has also contributed to my thinking on the structural and semantic aspects of the triggering of constructed opposites and their potential for being meaningful. I will therefore also draw extensively on Davies' work in what follows.

2.2 Earlier studies of opposition in context

Though there have been no previous studies of created opposition before Davies (2007, 2008) and this book, there are two important studies which inform the account being given here. These are Mettinger (1994) and Jones (2002). These researchers used corpus studies to investigate the contextual features of what Davies (2008), after Murphy (2002) labels 'canonical' antonyms. Neither of these foundational studies, therefore, is primarily interested in the discovery of how opposites might also be created in context. Davies (2008:17) describes them in the following terms:

However, so far, there have only been two major works whose sole focus is the study of textual oppositions. These are Mettinger

(1994) who explored opposites taken from a corpus of crime novels, and Jones (2002) who categorised common syntactic frames (e.g. *either* X *or* Y) in which opposites from a corpus of news texts co-occurred. Both studies claim to shed new light on theories of opposition by basing their findings on 'opposites in context' i.e. co-occurring oppositional pairs taken from their respective corpora. They both do however rely on the classic Saussurean qualitative distinction between language as a system ('langue') and language in use ('parole'), putting unjustified emphasis on the former when it comes to determining what constitutes a viable opposition.

I will return to Davies' comments on langue and parole later, but for now it should be noticed that he is making the point that both of these prior studies rely on pre-determined, or what Mettinger calls 'systemic' examples of opposites, rather than investigating those that are created by context. However, as we saw in Chapter One, Mettinger does recognize that such a process is possible.

We will return to the question of whether opposition is primarily a conceptual or a linguistic phenomenon, and how the two might be related in Chapter Five. For now, we can recognize that others working in this field have been aware of the contextual juxtaposition of non-canonical opposites without studying them in any depth. Jones' take on this potential for structures to create 'new' opposite relations is slightly different from Mettinger's. Jones (2002:154) takes a diachronic view of the potential for new members of the opposite class of semantic relations to be created by their co-occurrence in the regular contexts where canonical opposites are found:

> if antonyms occupy certain lexical environments in text, which other words also occupy those environments and could some of those words be seen as new, maturing antonyms?

What Jones fails to notice, apparently, is the potential for one-off opposites to be created in and by certain contexts, and for recipients of such texts to recognize them as analogous to the 'opposites' which they are more familiar with from their knowledge of the language in general. These are not, as Jones suggests, 'emerging' new opposites, but contextually relevant *temporary* associations of lexical items or longer stretches of text which encapsulate the producer's view of the phenomena related in this way. We saw two initial examples in Chapter One and will see many more in the remainder of this book, but as an illustration here, let us consider a further example from recent political events:

> And to all those watching tonight from beyond our shores, from parliaments and palaces to those who are huddled around radios in the forgotten corners of our world – our stories are singular, but our destiny is shared, and a new dawn of American leadership is at hand. (From U.S. President Obama's victory speech after the 2008 election results were announced[1])

During his campaign for the White House, Barack Obama was quickly recognized as an orator in the classical style, and he uses many of the rhetorical techniques that have been commented upon in relation to political speeches, such as three-part lists and parallel structures (Atkinson 1984). In addition, here he makes two juxtapositions intended to demonstrate the effect of his rise to power.

In the first instance he contrasts those in positions of power throughout the world with those lacking political power. He does so by the use of a syntactic frame *from X to Y* which would often include conventional opposites in the X and Y positions as in *from the rich to the poor* or *from east to west*. Here, however, he places two phrases in the X and Y position, creating an opposition between those in *parliaments and palaces* and *those who are huddled around radios in the forgotten corners of our world*. Note that this frame creates a gradable kind of opposition, implying as it does that it includes all those in-between the two extremes named. We will consider further the types of opposition created in context in the categories discussed below. For now we may note that it is important for Obama that he is not opposing these categories of people in order to align with one or the other, and this is evident from the opening of the sentence in which he explicitly addresses *all those watching tonight from beyond our shores*.

The other contextually created opposition occurs in the later part of the sentence where Obama says *our stories are singular, but our destiny is shared*. Here, he uses parallel structures (*X is Y*) with the Subject in each case being introduced by the possessive adjective *our.* These grammatical Subjects, then, are shown to have some similarity (they are 'ours'), though the head nouns in each case, *stories* (i.e. personal histories) and *destiny* (i.e. the future) are opposed by the disjunctive coordinator, *but*, between the two clauses. The initial part of the two clauses, then, just as in the advertisement for the UK Conservative Party examined in Chapter One, is set up as oppositional, being concerned with the past and the future respectively. What we then expect in the Complement position (after the copular verb, BE) is another contrast, which results in the reader being pre-disposed to see *singular* and *shared* as oppositional, though they do not form a conventional antonymous relationship linguistically in English. What Obama achieves so effectively by this device, which he uses again and again, is to demonstrate that he understands the things that divide people, but repeatedly overrides these in favour of seeing all human beings as facing the same problems.

What follows in the remainder of this chapter is an exploration of the contexts in which such constructed opposition takes form. The categories of context presented here are drawn from the three research projects mentioned above and the work of Davies (2008) but are influenced also by the foundational work of Mettinger and Jones in investigating the contexts in which conventional opposites regularly occur. The description which follows, however, is my own version of the categorization which all of us feel inclined to produce. Like many other category-based descriptions in linguistics, though, it is not made up of water-tight categories but has some more prototypical indicators of oppositional relations and some which are more peripheral.

2.3 Structural triggers of opposition

Before looking at the local textual effects in literary works (Chapter Three) and the discourse meanings in non-literary texts (Chapter Four), created by the exploitation of opposition in texts it is useful to see the range of ways in which oppositions are created and to try to develop a provisional typology of the syntactic means by which text producers can create textual opposition, though future work may demonstrate that there is no finite list of triggers for textually constructed opposites. The other issue discussed in this chapter is the relationship between purely structural triggers and those which are at least partially semantic in nature. I will return to this latter issue in the next section, though it is noteworthy that Mettinger (1994), Jones (2002) and Davies (2008) all treat syntactic and semantic triggers as manifestations of the same phenomenon and do not make a substantive distinction between them.

Before investigating the triggers of textual opposition in detail, let us consider the use of the term 'trigger' in this context. What is being proposed is a kind of link between the stable core of a language, the **langue,** and the fluctuating and malleable use of that language in context, the **parole.** It is currently fashionable for linguists to subscribe to the view that since the *langue* is clearly subject to change over time and susceptible to alteration in context, it therefore doesn't exist and usage – *parole* – is all we are left with. One of the hypotheses of this book is that such a wholesale rejection of Saussure's influential distinction is untenable. We will return to this argument later. In this case, the concept of semantic opposition, which is normally seen as a consistent lexical sense relation, may also be *textually produced* as a relationship which can be 'triggered' by a range of syntactic and semantic frames or co-textual clues. The origin of the term 'trigger' in pragmatics and its use in this context is commented upon by Davies:

> If oppositions are as omnipresent as Lyons, Cruse, Jones and so on believe, then it seems reasonable to assume that the common frames in which they appear will also structure the way we process non-canonical variations. These might work in the same way as what, in the field of pragmatics, Levinson (1983) calls 'presupposition-triggers'. Davies (2008:102–3)

At first sight there seem to be two different sorts of evidence that alert us to the presence of opposition in a text. These fall roughly into structural (grammatical) and semantic categories, although as we shall see, many of the examples have both structural and semantic features. This section illustrates the main categories of structural 'opposition-trigger' that was found in the data from the research projects mentioned above. In addition, I will discuss the findings of Davies (2008) which has refined our understanding of the syntactic triggers of opposition.

2.3.1 *Negation and related triggers*

Perhaps the likeliest candidate for the prototypical trigger of textual opposites is negation. There is a sense in which negation might be an odd choice for the most typical context of opposites, as Jones discovers that there are few such examples in his data. As Davies (2008:104–5) points out, this is mainly because with conventional opposites, the 'other' term is self-evident, meaning that where both are mentioned in an *X not Y* frame, the 'inclusion of the "*not Y*" elements merely acts to emphasise what on one level might be claimed to be tautological statements'. Thus, saying someone is *dead* implies that they are *not alive,* and saying that a meal is *not cooked* implies that it is *raw.* As Fellbaum (1995: 296) notes:

> in many instances the co-occurrence of semantically contrastive words in those frames is arguably redundant; one member of the pair would suffice to convey the intended information

But note that this redundancy is only present when the opposites concerned are mutually exclusive or complementary opposites. Thus, to say that a cup of tea is *not hot* does not imply that it is *cold,* and the context would probably lead us to conclude that it was *lukewarm* or some other such temperature between the extremes of this gradable antonymy.

What does tend to be the case with conventional opposites is that they occur in the *X not Y* frame when there is a reason to mention both terms of the opposition, for example when the contrast needs to be emphasized, as in the case of an answer to some explicit or implied accusation (*I'm not a coward, I'm very brave!*). In the case of constructed opposites, of course, both terms of the opposition need to be specified since they cannot be deduced from each other. Davies (2008:108–9) discusses the following example:

> We are *not* a colony, we are an equal and valued part of this nation. (*Daily Telegraph* 23rd September 2002 page 2)

This was spoken by Richard Burge, the chief executive to the Countryside Alliance, although it is unclear whether it was a speech to the crowd or spoken to the *Daily Telegraph* reporter. The colonizing force he refers to is the government and the oppressed are the rural folk who will be most affected by the new legislation. So these are in fact more conventional oppositional *concepts* being textually instantiated in a slightly less conventional way, owing to the trigger 'not'. The implication is that the city-based government representatives are riding roughshod over rural areas as if they were some kind of foreign invader. However, if the speaker had simply declared 'We are not a colony' it would be difficult to infer what comes after it, owing to its non-conventionality.

Later we will see examples where positive and negative parallel structures create opposition. Despite its relative rarity in conjunction with *conventional* opposites, the use of negation to *create* opposites appears to be ubiquitous and generally taken to indicate complementarity. In the following example from a poem, the negative and positive poles work with the semantics to describe a boy whose voice is breaking:

> He could *not* leave his own voice alone:
> He took it apart, he undressed it (McGuckian 1994:15)

McGuckian here sets up an interesting opposition between 'leaving something alone' and 'taking it apart'. Notice that conceptually there are a number of ways (i.e. a number of potential opposites) of not leaving something alone, including perhaps *interfere with, bother, fuss* etc. and she had a choice of how to evoke the strange voice the child grows through. The choice of *took it apart* implies that the voice is something separate from the child that he can investigate, the way that small children are inclined to do with their toys. The second version of the constructed opposite here, though, hints at the sexual nature of what is happening to him: *he undressed it.* As with earlier examples, the reader is presented with not only the normal semantics of *take it apart,* but the implied opposite of *leave alone* too, which evokes the self-obsessed nature of the adolescent boy. This is, therefore, one way of enriching the semantics of the poem economically which derives from the juxtaposition of two apparently unrelated phrases linked by their negative and positive polarities.

Although my interest in negation is in its capacity for constructing local textual oppositional meaning, there are others also interested in negation for its own sake whose viewpoint overlaps with mine. These include Hidalgo-Downing (2000:116), who relates negation to Werth's 'Text World Theory' (Werth 1999), claiming that negative propositions create unrealized subworlds which enable us to imagine things that are not happening. Hidalgo-Downing also links the cognitive effects of negation to schema theory, which hypothesizes that we understand the world around us by relating events to our stored experience of certain repeated patterns, such as what happens in a restaurant or doctor's surgery, which are known as 'schemata':

> Schemata are standardly defined as expectations; if negation is understood as the defeat of expectation, we can understand the relation between a negative and a positive term in terms of the relation between the schemata or frames evoked by each item. (Hidalgo-Downing 2000a:116)

The reporting of political news is rich in such negated opposites, as the 1997 British General Election data shows. The following extract demonstrates a contrast between politicians who keep their distance, and those who appear at least to be closer to the electorate:

> . . . let the professionals remember that the politicians that the public likes best are *not the aloof ones but the human ones.* (*Guardian* 1st May 1997 Editorial)

Although the created opposite, between *aloof* and *human,* is effectively set up by the negative structure, it also occurs in two parallel structures (*the X ones*) and these are contrasted using the conjunction *but.* These three triggers, then, seem to work together in this case, to persuade the reader to interpret the two juxtaposed words as opposites. Note that the creation of this particular opposition brings to the fore a common connotative, sense of the word *human*; to be warm and empathetic. This is not its central denotation out of context, but here the connotative elements come to the fore, encouraged by the constructed opposition relation in contrast with *aloof.* Juxtaposition which has such an effect of narrowing down the polysemous options is common in created opposites and demonstrates another interpretative tendency arising from opposition-creation. Those working on the discourse effects of negation specifically may well also point out here that the very mention of *aloof politicians,* even in a negated proposition, will conjure up such a person, possibly reinforcing the notion that it is, after all, *possible* for politicians to be aloof, since as Pagano says:

> . . . the set of propositions that could be denied in a given context is limited by the propositions which are experientially possible in that context (existential paradigm). We could then define *existential paradigm* as a set of assumptions which are experientially linked in a certain context. (Pagano 1994:255)

The significance of what Pagano indicates here is that speakers and writers cannot produce unlimited sets of negated propositions enumerating *all* the things that can't or won't happen. This leads to the cognitive result which is that we generally find it relatively easy to imagine negated propositions as if they were positive, since they are within the realm of possibilities for that context. I will return to this debate later, in discussing the potential ideological and/or literary effects of such constructions.

Though multiple triggers often seem to co-occur in this data, there are some examples where the negation is the *only* structural trigger of the created opposite:

> There is real enthusiasm for Labour. It's *not* just loathing for the Tories. (*Daily Mirror* 1st May 1997 Article)

This example does not use parallel structures or a conjunction, but relies on *not* and on the semantic evaluative (positive/negative) link between *enthusiasm* and *loathing* as well as the reader's schematic knowledge of British politics whereby *Labour* and *Tories* are opposed. These are not conventional opposites, but have enough semantic features in common, as well as having a positive and negative evaluation respectively, to be readily placed in opposition to each other.

There are a great many functionally similar examples in the 1997 election data, though many of them use not explicit negatives but other phrases which indicate that the two are incompatible:

> . . . election promises to build a 'new Jerusalem', a socialist Britain of 'fair shares for all' *in place of* Tory greed and selfishness. (*Daily Mail* 1st May 1997 Article)

> The grey man pinned his hopes on making the people love him; *instead* he has been stripped bare (*Guardian* 1st May 1997 Commentary)

The first of these examples uses the prepositional phrase *in place of* to indicate the incompatibility of the two alternative futures for Britain. The second uses the adverb *instead* to achieve the same effect. While these are not the same as negated opposites in structural terms, they do seem to work semantically in a rather similar way, as we can see by replacing their triggers by a negative:

> . . . election promises to build a 'new Jerusalem', a socialist Britain of 'fair shares for all' *not* Tory greed and selfishness.

> The grey man pinned his hopes on making the people love him; *not* strip him bare

Davies (2008:118) treats examples like these as a separate category of trigger, though his discussion demonstrates that he sees them as being more connected to negation than to comparative triggers, which Jones suggests as an option:

> Examples of unusual opposition in my data using the 'X *rather [than]* Y' frame have more in common with negation than comparison, as will be demonstrated in this section. However, I have found it useful to create a further category which sits functionally

somewhere in-between the negations and comparison. I call these 'Replacive' oppositions, borrowing the term from Quirk *et al's* (1972) *A Grammar of Contemporary English*. According to them a replacive 'expresses an alternative to what has preceded [it]' and that conjuncts such as 'rather' 'indicate that the proposed alternative is preferable' (1972:671–2). I have also included 'X *instead of* Y', (and 'X *in place of* Y') in this category. Jones includes this latter frame under 'Negated Antonymy' whereas Quirk et al note that 'instead' might also be treated as a replacive 'but more strongly implies a contrast'. (1972:672)

Clearly there is an argument for a separate category, but I am concerned here with the functional similarity between the negated and replacive opposites, which seem to create complementary opposites, where the mutual exclusivity of the two terms is assumed. If there is a difference between these examples, it may be that Davies' *replacives* imply a preference, whereas the X *not* Y frame may indicate a preference for either the positive over the negative term. I will return to these issues of their function in textual terms below (Section 2.5.2).

2.3.2 *Parallel structures*

The syntactic trigger of opposition that was most evident in the three research projects described above was the use of parallel structures. As pointed out in Chapter One, political slogans often use parallel structures for the purpose of creating opposition. The Conservative election slogan mentioned there, and the Larkin poem discussed in Jeffries (1993) and Section 1.1 indicate that parallel structures frequently form the context of opposition. As Leech (1969) points out:

Every parallelism sets up a relationship of equivalence between two or more elements . . . Interpreting the parallelism involves appreciating some external connection between these elements. The connection is, broadly speaking, a connection either of similarity or of contrast. (67)

The following poetic examples illustrate similar parallel structures which also each set up a non-conventional opposition:

> There is a plastic toy. There is no hope. (Duffy 1994:26)

> We have
> the language of stuffed birds, teacups. We don't have
> the language of bodies. (Duffy 1994:55)

In each case there is a repeated framework, one positive and one negative which indicates an opposition. In the first example *plastic toys* and *hope* are configured as the alternatives available to dolphins in captivity. Their plastic toys are the symbol of captivity, and they are in a mutually exclusive (complementary) relationship to *hope* which represents freedom. In the second example, the constructed opposition between *stuffed birds* and *teacups* represents the stiffness of an awkward teatime between two couples where one member of each partnership is having (or wishing to have) an affair with one of the other couple and *the language of bodies* represents the naturalness of their desires, which are not being fulfilled.

These examples demonstrate two features of created opposition. First, as we can see, the opposition does not have to be restricted to a sense relation between two single lexical items, but may relate two concepts that need phrases or even clauses to define them. This is not particularly surprising to anyone with knowledge of semantics where there are often phrases which equate to lexemes, though it does challenge our more everyday attitude to opposites, which are normally associated with lexemes.[2] More interesting theoretically is the fact that one of the interpretation processes that appears to be needed here, is the 'translation' of the created opposite into one that the reader is familiar with. In the first example, it becomes *freedom* and *captivity,* and in the second, *awkwardness* and *naturalness*. This dependency on langue-like relationships, already known by the reader lends more support to the need for some kind of relatively stable code upon which we depend for interpreting new texts, although the model would need to establish such a code as a changing and at least partly individualized one.

Other examples based on parallel structures go further by using ellipsis to indicate the deep predictability of the parallelism:

> with the rage
> Of one moment, the contentment of the next (McGuckian 1994:30)

> He is concerned with volume, space.
> I with the next meal. (Duffy 1994:20)

In both of these examples, there are parallel structures indicating a contrast of some sort, but with one element of the parallel structure missing in the second version. In the first example it is a noun that is missing (i.e. *the next **moment***) and in the second it is a verb (i.e. ***I am concerned** with the next meal*). Note that unlike in the previous set of examples, the parallel structure works alone to indicate opposite status here, there being no negation. The first example is from a poem where McGuckian describes the feelings of a woman abandoned by her husband who alternates between *rage* and *contentment,* which though not a conventional opposite, is nevertheless recognizable as familiar extremes of negative and positive emotion respectively. In the latter, the created opposition between *volume/space* and *the next meal* leaves us with a strong impression of opposition between the *abstract* art of the painter and the *concrete* hunger of his sitter, meaning that a translation into a conventional opposite is quite easy to make.

Note that there is the potential here for the charge of interpretative positivism (see Chapter One), but I am not claiming that parallel structures *always* indicate opposition. As Short (1996:15) points out in his discussion of parallelism in literary work, it 'has the power not just to foreground parts of a text for us, but also to make us look for parallel or contrastive meaning links between those parallel parts'. The question of whether readers or hearers may search for contrast or similarity will depend partly on the semantic content of the parallel structures themselves. We have seen examples already where one part of the parallel structure contains a conventional opposite and this sets up the expectation of a further contrast in another part of the structure.

There is thus normally a semantic element to the text which clinches the diagnosis of a created opposite occurring, but there may also be a potential explanatory mechanism for these oppositions deriving from pragmatics. This is pragmatic presupposition (Simpson 1993:127–8) or conventional implicature (Grice 1975:44–45) which perhaps forms the interface between the *langue* and *parole* that I am arguing for. Thus, our awareness of the tendency for parallel structures to contain conventional opposites as their main point of difference may predispose us towards reading parallel structures with no such conventional oppositions in a contrasting way. The two examples above do not depend on conventional opposites, though they each have a supplementary pair of words (*one/the next* and *he/I*) which may be seen as priming the reader to interpret the main lexical items as oppositional.

I have noted that the parallel structures frequently operate in conjunction with negation as triggers of opposition, but this is not necessary to their interpretation as opposites. The following are some examples from reporting of the 1997 British General Election in the *Times* newspaper on 1st May. The first uses both parallel structure and also negation, the second only parallel structure:

Not to vote in this, or any, election is not *a statement.* It is *a failure.*

We took *coffee,* in industrial quantities, Mr Blair, as usual, took *nothing for granted.*

The oppositions in these cases are not conventional, though again, the interpretation process may result in readers mapping them onto more familiar opposites. The use of *statement,* for example, opposed to *failure* in this context, might therefore be interpreted as equivalent to *success*; in other words, a strong, positive action. This example demonstrates one of the possible clues to how we may interpret the constructed opposite; if one of the terms is 'normally' paired with a different opposite, the latter becomes the basis of interpretation of the 'new' one. Thus although we know the meaning of *statement* here, we embellish it in opposition to *failure* with the idea that it is a statement that would denote success if it weren't being denied. The import of this extract is that not voting is a negative force. In the second example, we have a contrast between drinking a great deal of coffee, which is associated with trying to keep energy levels up, and the apparent capacity of Tony Blair to continue working without a break while there is a chance of failure. This is achieved by simply juxtaposing the two sets of people – Blair the infallible against news reporters who need their rest.

2.3.3 *Coordination*

All of the coordinating conjunctions seem to be available as indicators of opposition in certain contexts, although the contrastive ones, *but, or* and *yet* are more obviously inclined to opposition than *and*. Jones (2002:61–74) finds coordination a pervasive context for his conventional antonyms as over 38 per cent of his examples include some kind of coordinator. We could argue that through frequency of occurrence, the disjunctive *but* and *or* (plus some other rarer cases) produce conventional implicatures of oppositeness, as in the following examples:

> I find this difficult, *and then again* easy,
> as I watch him push his bike off in the rain. (Duffy 1994:19)

> You kicked him, *but* stared
> at your parents, appalled, when you got back home. (Duffy 1994:68)

There are probably other ways of classifying *and then again,* but here it seems to be synonymous with *but,* so I have included it as a contrastive conjunction. In this example, the opposition between *difficult* and *easy* is a conventional one, although we will see later that it is not being used in a straightforward way. The opposition in the second example (*kicked* vs. *stared*) is more obviously new, indicating that one reaction to learning as a child how babies are made, is to kick the person who told you, indicating that you do not believe it. The other reaction, which may happen in conjunction with the disbelief, is to believe it and try to imagine your parents doing it! The apparent opposites here, *kicked* and *stared,* are really indicative, then, of *disbelief* and *belief;* a more conventional opposite.

Davies (2008) introduces the category of Contrastive opposition to cover this use of the conjunction *but,* though he points out that it has some overlap with the category he has labelled 'Concessive' opposition (while, despite etc). The latter is not represented in my own data, but as Davies (2008:118) points out, there is a difference between the contrastive presentation of constructed opposites each side of a conjunction and those which are introduced by a concessive, a term he borrows from Quirk *et al.* 1972:

> One kind of syntactic feature which is largely ignored by Mettinger and Jones is what Quirk et al. (1972) call the 'concessive conjunct'. Examples of these include '*while*', '*despite*', '*yet*', '*(al)though*' and '*however*'. The 'concessive clauses' in which these conjuncts feature, according to Quirk et al., 'imply a contrast between two circumstances; i.e. that in the light of the circumstance in the dependant clause, that in the main clause is surprising' (1972:745). Elsewhere they claim that concessives 'signal the unexpected, surprising nature of what is being said in view of what was said before that' (1972:674).

Although *and* is not so predictably a sign of opposition, it does occur in some examples, usually alongside other triggers and/or a more clearly 'semantic' opposition as indicated by the choice of vocabulary or the general semantic context. In the following extract from newspaper reporting of the 1997 British general election, the first sentence sets up an opposition based on the notion of a *battle* using *but* to indicate the oppositional frame, and the second sentence repeats this using the near-synonym *struggle*. These words summon the prepositional frame '*between X and Y*' where the conjunction *and* is used with another, prepositional, trigger *between*, in a very particular context of opposition:

> There was a real battle in this election campaign, but it had not much to do with that between the parties. It was a struggle between *packaging* and *content,* between *politicians as soap powder* and *parties as vehicles for informed debate.* (*Financial Times* 1st May 1997 Editorial)

The result in this case is a complementary opposite. The use of *between* in the context of the specific lexemes *battle* and *struggle* sets up mutually exclusive opposites, because in battles, only one side can win. Politicians, then, will be seen only as another consumer product (*packaging; politicians as soap powder*) or as people with a message (*content*), not both. As we shall see later, in other contexts, *between* can also introduce gradable opposites.

Note that one of the functions of the conjunction *and* in introducing created opposites is to put forward the notion that despite being opposites, and thus stereotypically mutually exclusive, there is sometimes a paradoxical co-existence of the two extremes:

> The wedge-shaped room *compressing*
> Me and *stretching* me, I felt
> Something . . . (McGuckian 1994:47)

This is not the same as categorizing them as converses, since they are not simply two perspectives on the same phenomenon but are conflicting but co-existent states that logically should not be able to co-exist. In the next example, Duffy explores the feelings of a couple confronted by the adultery of one of them and she indicates that despite the lack of linguistic communication (*dumb*), the flowers sent for no apparent reason still succeed in communicating guilt:

> You're an expert, darling; your flowers
> *dumb and explicit* on nobody's birthday. (Duffy 1994:120)

In both of these cases, a relatively conventional conceptual opposition (*squash* vs. *stretch* and *communicative* vs. *non-communicative*) has been lexicalized in a slightly unusual way, but more importantly the opposition has been undermined by their co-occurrence, which is indicated by *and*.

2.3.4 Comparatives

The use of comparative structures to set up opposition is recognized by others (see Mettinger 1994 and Jones 2002) as one of the standard contexts in which conventional opposites occur, so it would not be surprising to find created examples in similar contexts:

what they ask of women is *less* their bed,
Or an hour between two trains, *than* to be almost gone,
Like the moon that turns her pages day by day. (McGuckian 1994:14)

Each lighted
Window shows me cardiganed, *more* desolate
Than the garden, and *more* hallowed
Than the hinge of the brass-studded
Door that we close . . . (McGuckian 1994:19)

The constructions *less . . . than . . .* and *more . . . than . . .* imply some kind of gradable opposition. In the first example this construction indicates that women are indeed wanted for *their bed,* but that more than this, they are required *to be almost gone.* I will discuss the meaning of such examples in more detail in Chapter Three, but for now we should note that this seems to be both setting up an opposition and acknowledging the co-existence of the two opposed terms, as we saw in the coordinated examples in the last section. Thus, the poem claims that women are wanted for sex, for which they would need, at a minimum, to be physically present, but the contrast made is with not being present (to be almost gone) and this, it is claimed, is desired more even than sexual satisfaction. Thus, the gradability is set up between being present (i.e. having sex) and being absent, and the claim is made that women are expected to be near the absent end of the range, though presumably close enough to be used for sexual gratification. A similar situation occurs in the second example, where the garden is clearly *desolate,* though the narrator is more so, and the door is *hallowed,* though the narrator is more so. These words can be read as opposites in that *desolate* has negative and *hallowed* positive connotations. Nevertheless, the speaker is both at once and is again simultaneously setting up and demolishing the opposition.

The news data (from the 1997 British General Election) throws up similar examples, where comparative constructions seem be setting up an opposition:

> But redistribution will be *more* about creating opportunity *than* it will be about taking a few quid off one group of people and giving it to other people on benefit (*Guardian* 1st May 1997 Interview)

> Most of the troublemakers seemed *less* moved by ideological grievance *than* by the thrill of shoving someone famous and being rude on TV. (*Guardian* 1st May 1997 Article)

> But parties are *more* than hucksters, just as citizens are *more* than consumers. (*Independent* 1st May 1997 Editorial)

These examples share the potential to be interpreted as gradable, though in the context of politics, this is sometimes as close as you get to truly acknowledging the 'middle-ground'. The examples work in just the same way as the poetic ones, using the range implied by the comparative form to indicate that there is an incremental possibility here and that the situations described cover both the 'lower' end of the spectrum and also some points higher up.

2.4 Lexical triggers of opposition

Although many of the triggers for opposition are structural as shown in the last section, I have made a number of references to the contribution of semantics to the created oppositions in question. While some of the structural features can 'create' opposition without obvious semantic help, many of the examples I have come across are at least partly dependent on the meanings of some of the lexemes chosen in the context. Some of the following categories are recognized in the work of Jones (2002) and Davies (2008), though they both consider the different contexts of opposition as equivalent, and do not distinguish between structural and lexical aspects of these contexts. However, in view of the significance of conventional opposites in helping to create unconventional ones in context, it seems helpful to separate out those features of constructed opposition which depend on lexical choice rather than structural choices.

2.4.1 *Explicit mention of oppositional relation*

The first category of example with this kind of semantic support includes those where a verb is chosen whose semantics set up some kind of contrast. These might include, for example, *compare, change, transform.* The contrast is then usually played out in the clause elements following the verb:

> your body in the semi-gloom
> *Turning* my dead layers into something
> Resembling a rhyme. (McGuckian 1994:16)

To *change* from a bum
to a billionaire. (Duffy 1994:121)

A rare flash of emotion from a man who has *turned* cynicism into an art form (*Express* 1st May 1997 Article)

The 'evil genius' behind the strategy that has *turned* the party from unelectable to unstoppable in 10 years. (*Express* 1st May 1997 Article)

What we have in these examples is some evidence that poetry and political reporting use the same strategies, and manage to summarize whole arguments in the 'soundbite' of a created opposite. Most striking, perhaps, are the two alliterative examples where *bum* and *billionaire* on the one hand and *unelectable* and *unstoppable* on the other are placed in opposition to each other. The latter, particularly, steps around an expected opposite where *electable* would be the opposite of *unelectable,* and produces not a complementary, but a gradable opposition, whereby *electable* falls halfway between the extremes of *unelectable* and *unstoppable.* We will return to the potential for changing or manipulating the categories of opposite in the next chapter.

This category is similar to that labelled **Distinguished Antonymy** by Jones (2002:81–85) and **Explicit Opposition** by Davies (2008:129):

> Occasionally, texts utilise oppositional pairs through triggers which *explicitly* draw attention to their contrastive function. In my data, again the contrasts are often between whole scenarios rather than just individual words. The clearest examples are those which use phrases such as 'X *contrast(ed) with* Y' or 'X *opposite/opposed to* Y'.

Davies draws attention to the fact that whereas Jones' examples make assumptions about the conventional oppositional nature of the lexical items concerned, his own construct opposition where no such relation is presumed. Both make the point that there is something 'metalinguistic' about the explicit mentioning of opposition or contrast, as we see here in Jones (2002:82):

> Though all six sentences are metalinguistic in the sense that a distinction between antonyms is overtly referred to, it is important to note that the focus of these examples is always on the difference arising between antonyms, not on the antonyms themselves.

A similar phenomenon is the use of explicit and self-conscious devices to draw the reader's attention to the fact that an opposition is being set up. This can happen in a number of ways, as we can see from the following examples in the 1997 election data:

> The 'radical centre' is the verbal ground where he has finally located the party. He insists it is not *an oxymoron*. . . . For the centre was the only place you could build a consensus. How, then, could it be truly radical? (*Guardian* 1st May 1997 Interview)

> This game of mirrors makes campaigning difficult for Ashdown, *treading that fine line* between aspiration and realism (*Guardian* 1st May 1997 Article)

> A combination of the leader's will and his ability to impose it on his party – *such a contrast* with the 'drift' and 'division' of the Tories, for which Blair shows a deeply felt contempt (*Guardian* 1st May 1997 Article)

These writers have taken words and phrases that explicitly label ideas as opposites, such as *oxymoron, treading a fine line* and *contrast*. These words become the framework for setting up oppositions between *radical* and *centre*; *aspiration* and *realism* and *the leader's will and his ability to impose it* and *'drift' and 'division'* respectively. Not all such examples use metalanguage (e.g. *oxymoron*), though many do.

We may not be surprised to find such explicit awareness of opposition in the political news writers, but it is common also in the openings of novels, as we see from the following examples:

With *a double edge* of helplessness and rage (Cornwell 2000:1)

He might have searched Europe over for *a greater contrast between* juxtaposed scenes (Hardy 1891:1)

In the first example, Cornwell tells us that these emotions (*helplessness* and *rage*) are to be read as opposed, though probably both present together. In the second example, Hardy expresses the view that the two scenes he is describing, a *deserted edifice* and *the steam round-abouts* should be seen as contrasted by the reader who has to then work out in what sense they are opposed.

Chapter Three will return to issues of the meanings and effects of constructed opposites in literary contexts, where many of Jones' comments on what he here calls the 'focus' of his examples will become relevant. For now, it is worth noting that his contention that explicit mentioning of antonymy is 'metalinguistic' gives some support to my argument that the concept of oppositeness – and possibly its linguistic counterpart in antonyms – is a cognitive reality for text producers and recipients.

2.4.2 *Influence of conventional opposites in context*

As we have seen in a number of the examples given so far, created or constructed opposites are often not far textually from a pair of more conventional opposites, or pairs of words that translate easily into a more conventional opposite pairing. Let us consider again one of the examples used earlier:

> There was a real battle in this election campaign, but it had not much to do with that between the parties. It was a struggle between *packaging* and *content,* between *politicians as soap powder* and *parties as vehicles for informed debate.*

Here, the relatively conventional opposition between packaging and content add to the effect of the words battle and struggle discussed above, so that by the time the reader reaches the politicians as soap powder versus parties as vehicles for informed debate opposition, it is easy to assimilate.

The relative frequency of conventional oppositions in the context of created ones, and the tendency for the analyst and possibly also the reader, to interpret constructed opposites in relation to conventional pairings, raise the question of whether there are in fact certain more fundamental oppositional pairings that underlie all constructed ones, and are thus psychologically prior to those that readers are decoding in context. This question will require a different kind of research to answer, and the further issue of whether such fundamental opposites are also universal, and thus possibly absolute in some way, is a philosophical question which requires still different kinds of investigation. I return to this topic in Chapter Five.

At the other extreme from explicit or metalinguistic comment is what I am calling auto-evocation. This rather grand term defines a technique of invoking an oppositional relationship by the use of only *one* of the relevant terms. It depends, of course, on the reader knowing the alternative, much like the invoking of a word by a familiar collocate, and so it tends to be most relevant to conventional opposition. The mechanism by which this summoning up of an opposite works could be described in Gricean (1975) terms, as flouting the maxim of Quantity, by providing too little information, but thereby invoking a conventional relationship of opposition. As we see from the following example from *Sula*, a novel by Toni Morrison, the opposition which is evoked by one of the oppositional terms is often related in context to other, created oppositions:

> It is called the suburbs now, but when *black* people lived there it was called the Bottom. (Morrison 1982:1)

The use of deictic *when* refers to an earlier time and might therefore be contrasted with its near-opposite *now.* This frame brings the phrase *black people* into a situation where there is a pragmatic presupposition that the opposite of *black* is relevant now, and thus leads the reader to draw the conclusion that it is now the white people who live there. Note that in addition to the *when* and *now* opposite, and the *black/white* opposite, there is a third, created opposition in this sentence, between the term *suburbs* and the name *the Bottom,* with all the negative implications of the latter term. Semantically, it could be argued that there is no unambiguous reference to white people, but this is highly unlikely as the semantic loading of the opposites within the text itself, and the schematic knowledge of most readers, would make the evocation of white people almost unavoidable.

Examples of auto-evocation are not restricted to the openings of novels, as this example from the 1997 election data attests:

> *On paper,* Putney should be a *safe* Tory seat (*Financial Times* 1st May Article)

This sentence evokes the *safe/unsafe* opposition which is regularly used in election debates, but without mentioning the *unsafe* part of the relationship. Interestingly, the sentence's force is, effectively, that the seat is indeed *unsafe,* though this is not explicitly part of its proposition. The opposite in this case is invoked by another auto-evoked opposition, *on* paper, coupled with the modal verb phrase, *should be.* The effect of this coupling is that the reader will summon up by pragmatic presupposition not what *should be,* but what *is,* and this will be lined up with the opposite of *on paper,* which is *in reality,* and the opposite of *safe,* which is *unsafe.*

2.5 Meanings and local textual functions of constructed opposition

In the above account of the triggers of textually created opposition, I have sometimes touched upon the local relevance of the examples discussed, and I have taken for granted that the reader is familiar with some kind of generalized notion of oppositeness, and in some cases with particular sub-types of opposition, based on logical properties. Before we consider in more detail the contextual effects of such examples (Chapters Three and Four), it is worth considering the generalized meaning potential of oppositeness triggered in this way.

In Chapter One, I referred to the 'problem' of interpretative positivism, which Simpson (1993:113) dismisses on the grounds that there is some kind of 'common denominator' in many of the stylistic features which he and others have examined. The same kind of question, of course, hangs over the phenomenon that is the focus of this book, though perhaps the creation of opposites gives us an insight into the kind of meaning Simpson was referring to by his phrase 'common denominator'. Thus, if we consider a pair of invented opposites which are triggered by the same kind of mechanism, but have rather different content, we may be able to see how the layers of meaning build up:

> There was no hurry. There were scones for tea.
> There was no shame. There were expenses to claim.

These examples use exactly the same triggers, parallel structures and negation, to create oppositions between *hurry* and *scones* in the first case and *shame* and *expenses* in the second. In both cases, of course, there are underlying conventional opposites that can be referred to in interpreting them. Thus, in the first case, the reader will draw upon the opposite of hurry (go slowly) in thinking about why scones would be identified with lack of speed. Cultural knowledge of this particular kind of cake and its associations with relaxed tea times (probably in a British context) would allow the detailed opposition to be constructed, leading to the interpretation that if there were scones available, no other pressure would be enough to make those concerned hurry. The second example works on a different topic (probably the scandal of politicians' expenses currently raging in the UK) but it works in exactly the same kind of way. Thus, the first term, *shame* is known to be opposite to *integrity,* and the reader is led to the conclusion that claiming money (expenses) is so important that it has to be re-classified as part of integrity, not shame.

Though there is a perceived tendency to see constructed opposites as stereotypically complementary (mutually exclusive), this is not a universal tendency, and the triggers themselves may contribute to the interpretation which is most likely in some cases. Thus, the use of negation, parallelism, explicit and replacive triggers usually result in complementary opposition, but others, such as comparatives, may produce gradable opposites and transitional triggers will often produce directional oppositions. The significance of such different outcomes will depend on the content and context in each case, and in many cases there will need to be some inferencing effort on the part of the reader, to construct a reasonable meaning from the created opposition in its textual context. Some of these issues will be discussed in Chapter Five.

3

Literary effects of constructed opposition

3.1 Introduction – opposites in literary works

Chapter Two discussed the contextual construction of opposition by grammatical and semantic means. The meaning of some of the examples was discussed as part of the analysis to establish types of created oppositions. In this chapter, and the one that follows, meaning or function becomes the primary focus and I investigate the effects or contextual meanings of the examples I have found in literature (this chapter) and in the news (Chapter Four).

As we shall see, there are a number of similarities between literary and non-literary texts in the way that they create semantic relations of opposition between words, phrases, clauses (and at times longer stretches of text) and the common factors in this meaning-making have been explored to some extent in the previous chapter. Here, I will consider the specifically literary aspects of unconventional opposites, and their potential effect on interpretative practices.

It may be helpful here to consider Culler's (1975) notion of 'literary competence' as one of the factors in the interpretation of constructed opposites. Culler's view was that our ability to interpret literary works is a second-order semiotic process which depends on the first order linguistic ability acquired primarily through speaking a language. Learning to understand literature requires the acquisition of further rules for interpretation, as Culler points out:

> . . . its formal and fictional qualities bespeak a strangeness, a power, an organization, a permanence which is foreign to ordinary speech. Yet the urge to assimilate that power and permanence or to let that formal organization work upon us requires us to make literature into a communication, to reduce its strangeness . . . (Culler 1975:134)

This similarity between the basic material of literature and everyday language is one of the findings of this study. While we may see more challenging and 'strange' constructions of opposites in poetry, the exact same mechanism for producing a new semantic relation of this sort seems to be used also in news reporting and other more mundane functional texts. What these created opposites signify in context will depend upon the genre and the content of the specific example, as well as many more contextual factors including the prior knowledge and background of the reader/hearer etc.

What Culler's notion suggests to me specifically in relation to the subject matter of this book is that our understanding of the general – if fluctuating – relations of oppositeness between lexical items in our knowledge of a language underpins and allows for the interpretation of new opposites in literary contexts. This process will be demonstrated in the rest of this chapter by three detailed studies of literary texts and their unconventional opposites. The first is the study of McGuckian's and Duffy's poetry already introduced in Chapter Two. The second is a detailed analysis of a single Philip Larkin poem, 'Talking in Bed' and the third is a study of the openings of one hundred novels.

3.2 Opposition-creation in the poems of Mebdh McGuckian and Carol Ann Duffy

In Chapter One I made a comparison between the argument that poetry needs to be dependent on regular patterning of language in order to successfully deviate from this patterning and the argument that we need conventional opposites to interpret unconventional ones. I would argue, therefore, that although the construction of new and surprising opposites is in itself an undermining of the 'langue-bound' notion of opposition as a sense relation belonging to words themselves, the existence of the idea of opposition is also vital to this innovative process. Just like the Gothic novel which can undermine divisions between established oppositions (like life and death) only because such divisions are generally perceived to exist, the created oppositions of textual data depend to a certain extent on the reader construing them as analogous to the conventional oppositions of the langue. This process works not only for the whole category of opposition, but also for its sub-categories, as we shall see.

The four sub-types of opposition introduced in Chapter One are to be found, even among created opposites:

> your body in the semi-gloom
> Turning my dead layers into something
> Resembling a rhyme. (McGuckian 1994:16)

McGuckian's description of (partial?) sexual satisfaction in this example sets up an opposition between *dead layers* (the narrator's unresponsive body?) and *a rhyme* (her aroused body). However, instead of leaving the opposition at that, where it would most likely be interpreted as a complementary opposite, leaving no other possibilities but these two, she acknowledges the gradable nature of such pleasure when she downplays the effect with the phrase *something resembling*.

The small number of directional opposites in the data are relatively conventional as can be seen from the following example:

> I *swooped*, pincered the world in my beak, then *soared* (Duffy 1994:32)

While it might not be one of those opposites that spring to mind like *hot-cold*, the contrast between *swoop* and *soar*, once pointed out, seems obvious. Neither is it being used in a particularly challenging way here, since the verbs are applied to a bird and they follow each other in the way that you would expect of directional opposites, just like the *wrap-unwrap* that occurs later in the same poem.

Complementary opposites are more frequent than antonyms in poetry, with Duffy introducing a new complementary opposite in her exploration of what it feels like to be an immigrant to England:

> For a moment
> you are there, in the other country, knowing its name.
> And then a desk. A newspaper. A window. English rain. (Duffy 1994:90)

Here the *other country* is incompatible to, and therefore a complementary of, the list of items in the final line which are evocative of life in England. Notice that there are four items in the list (*desk, newspaper, window, rain*) which mimic the movement of the eyes away from a near focus such as one might have when daydreaming; a mental 'escape' from the situation, only to find the rain making it difficult to imagine the other country after all.

Duffy's contemplation of the *other country* causes her to muse on the nature of the emigré's feelings about their homeland. One of the recurrent observations she makes is that it is hard to distinguish between memories of the place and anticipation of seeing it again. In making this observation she twice creates an opposition that seems to work like converseness, where the contrasting terms represent two approaches to what is essentially the same situation:

> The other country, is it *anticipated* or *half-remembered* (Duffy 1994:89)
>
>   tugging uselessly on *memory*
> or *hope*. (Duffy 1994:76)

In both of these extracts the focus is *the other country,* and Duffy seems to be asserting that both ways of approaching it (i.e. looking backward and looking forward) amount to the same thing. This kind of manipulation of the reader's expectations and normal understanding of opposites is common in the poetry I have investigated. It may, indeed, be one of the distinguishing factors of poetic construction of opposites as opposed to news reporting or other similar discourses where the creation of opposition is more subtle because it is less clearly challenging to the status quo.

It is part of the definition of converseness that the two parts of the opposition co-exist, which is why I have characterized the last two examples as converses. There are also examples, however, of directional opposites and complementaries where, despite the fact that they are mutually exclusive (i.e. complementary) by definition, the two terms of the opposition are apparently also co-existent. For example, Duffy creates unconventional complementaries which she then partially undermines by allowing the mutually exclusive terms of the opposition to co-exist. Two such examples deal in one case with missing a loved one and in the other with memories of how her mother speaks:

This is *pleasurable*. Or shall I cross that out and say it is *sad*? (Duffy 1994:86)

Only tonight
I am *happy* and *sad*
like a child
who stood at the end of the summer
and dipped a net
in a green, erotic pond (Duffy 1994:88)

In both of these cases, the co-existing opposition tries to capture the kind of sweet melancholy that allows us to feel what are normally perceived to be contradictory emotions at once. In both cases there is a loved person involved and thinking about them is presumably the cause of the positive feelings, though absence and distance (in time/ space?) cause the sadness in each case respectively.

A more subtle, but nevertheless quite radical subversion of opposition occurs in examples where the context effects a change of sub-category, allowing the (normally conventional) opposition to be viewed in a different way. Since these examples may occur in either direction between each pair of sub-categories, I have grouped them, rather arbitrarily, by their 'home' sub-category that is antonymy, complementarity and directional opposites. There were no examples in the data of converses converting to another type of opposition, although they do occur as the target category.

In the poem 'Mean Time', Duffy chooses to combine a directional opposition *shorten-lengthen* with two complementary pairs *endless-finite* and *day-night*. In the process, she creates a new, converse relationship for this context, which accurately characterizes the winter solstice as a simultaneous reduction in the day and a lengthening (to infinity) of the night:

> These are the shortened days
> and the endless nights. (Duffy 1994:26)

The use of only one of each of the pairs *lengthen-shorten* and *endless-finite* here means that the two pairs are put into a paradigmatic relationship which causes the reader to almost blend the two oppositional meanings together. Thus, we are at once confronted with the process of days getting shorter (and thus nights getting longer which is only implied) and the fact of the nights seeming to last forever (and days thus being far too short – finite). The effect is both symmetry and lack of it: the days are presented as getting ever shorter while the nights are already interminable. The perspective of a person living through a winter in the northern hemisphere is captured here; though we know that the process is symmetrical, it is hard to believe at times.

The number of examples where complementaries are converted to other categories may reflect the greater frequency of complementaries more generally, but it is noticeable that these examples occur more in poetry than in the election reporting data. Both poets provided examples of a number of such conversions. We saw an example earlier where McGuckian undermines the absolute nature of the complementary relationship by converting it into a gradable antonymy:

> Each lighted
> Window shows me cardiganed, *more* desolate
> *Than* the garden, and *more* hallowed
> *Than* the hinge of the brass-studded
> Door that we close . . . (McGuckian 1994:19)

Another similar example is as follows:

> Perhaps she purchased, by this biblical
> Applique, *less* a genuine daylight

Than the aplomb of those winter-white insets
On my edge-to-edge bolero. . . . (McGuckian 1994:21)

The comparative structures in these extracts achieve a gradable effect where there would normally be an assumption of complementaries. Thus, *desolate–hallowed,* though not conventional, is nevertheless recognizably made up of absolutes, which can only be opposed to their lack. The other pair, *genuine–aplomb,* is also unconventionally opposed here, and is made up of one term which has a conventional opposite (*genuine/false*) and one term, *aplomb,* which generally is not seen as part of an opposite pairing. Interestingly, the latter term is here put into the position where we would expect false, and it thus takes on the negative connotations of that word. Rather like the potential for other positively valued words such as plausible to take on an edge in certain contexts, this use rings hollow. Aplomb is something that we may sometimes admire, but in the context of this poetry, full of a sense of loss, it strikes us as arrogant and within the created opposition, false.

There begins to be a relativity about such concepts in the presence of intensifiers like *more* and *less,* which leads to the potential for questioning all absolute values. It is, perhaps, not surprising that it is mostly poets who question the incompatibles, and convert them to gradable concepts. In Chapter Five, we will consider what would happen if this process were more common in politics and journalism.

It is, of course, also possible to change complementaries to directional opposites, as in the following example from a poem written in the voice of a baby:

They wrap
and unwrap me, a surprise they want to have again (Duffy 1994:35)

Here, we have a conventional reversive opposite, *wrap-unwrap,* which provides the interpretative context for reinterpreting the complementary relationship between *surprise* and its opposite (lack of surprise) as a directional opposite *surprise-again.* Thus, like wrapping and unwrapping, the surprise can be wiped out by reversing the direction, allowing the surprise to happen again. This is something that children indeed seem to perceive differently from adults, as they enjoy games like 'Peek-a-boo' with their carers from a young age, though the adults involved normally find the child's hilarity alien, though charming.

The final example of conversion from complementaries to be discussed here is from one of Duffy's poems which is written in the voice of the neighbours of the child Jesus:

> Our wives
> were first resentful, then superior. (Duffy 1994:51)

The opposition *resentful-superior* is built on a combination of a complementary relationship, *resentful-content,* and a converse, *superior-inferior.* I would argue, however, that here it is the converse relationship that wins out in this context where the situation (the presence of the precocious child-wonder Jesus) does not alter, but the attitude of the neighbours changes from looking up to Mary and Joseph to looking down on them. The implication is, in all cases where two relatively conventional opposites are invoked, that the two 'missing' halves are also implied. Thus, the women in this example started off as *resentful* because they felt *inferior* and ended up *content* because they felt *superior.* The economy of such amalgamations of two sets of opposites, of course, suits the poetic mode in particular.

3.3 Larkin's 'Talking in Bed' – questioning the world in poetry

The second case study presents an analysis of a poem by Philip Larkin, called 'Talking in Bed'. Previous chapters have included a number of poetic examples of textual construction of opposition, and these have illustrated local effects of a number of different kinds of opposition-construction. Here, rather than picking out only the occasional opposition, I wish to demonstrate the possibilities that arise when the questioning of – and repeated (re-)construction of – opposites forms the major part of the meaning of a poem. Section 3.2 refers to one of the early examples of textual construction of opposites that I found, also in a Philip Larkin poem, where the construction of a paradigm of time based on two sets of opposites (*now-always* and *now-then*) was finally resolved in favour of these opposites being false anyway. The current poem is a later, and more complex, example of a poetic text being largely dependent on the play that Larkin makes with conventional, and unconventional, opposites.

Here is the poem in full:

Talking in Bed

  1 Talking in bed ought to be easiest,
Lying together there goes back so far,
An emblem of two people being honest.

Yet more and more time passes silently.
  5 Outside, the wind's incomplete unrest
Builds and disperses clouds about the sky,

And dark towns heap up on the horizon.
None of this cares for us. Nothing shows why
At this unique distance from isolation

10 It becomes still more difficult to find
Words at once true and kind
Or not untrue and not unkind. (Larkin 1964:29)

If we consider the poem in sequence, the first line has a superlative form, which implicitly constructs some kind of opposite from what is said here to be *easiest.* The reader may contemplate the different options for what is implied to be less easy, and these are likely to focus on part of the clausal subject; either *talking* or in *bed.* In other words, the superlative form implies comparison, and in the absence of explicit grounds of comparison, we are left to conjecture what that may be. Readers' experience of other texts will not incline them to assume that the inexplicit comparison is with some completely different activity, such as *talking in bed ought to be easier than driving a train.* Thus, the tendency may well be to consider the alternatives to *talking*, which at their simplest would be *not talking*, though other activities typical of being in bed, such as *having sex* or *sleeping* may also spring to mind, and *in bed,* which may compare with any number of places, such as *in the kitchen, at the theatre* or *on the beach.* At this point, then, and ignoring for now the unlikely options (e.g. *talking in bed ought to be easier than riding an elephant)* the reader has the following possible interpretations of the first line available:

1   talking in bed ought to be easier than not talking in bed

2   talking in bed ought to be easier than doing other things in bed

3   talking in bed ought to be easier than talking elsewhere

The next two lines use a kind of apposition or reiteration of the Subject to equate lying in bed with being honest:

Subject	Predicator	Adverbial	Subject
Lying together there	goes	back so far,	An emblem of two people being honest.

What we seem to have so far, then, is equivalence being set up between lying in bed and being honest, and the implicature that this honesty ought to also equate to talking. Note also, of course, that there is a pun on lying, which also hints at the opposite of honesty, telling lies. The reader may, however, already be aware that things are not as they should be, because of the use of the deontic modal, *ought to,* which implies that what should be the case is not.

The beginning of the next stanza opens with confirmation of this doubt, when the disjunct *yet* introduces the information by conventional implicature (Grice 1975) that indeed, the couple concerned are not speaking in bed very much (*more and more time passes silently).* The semantic relation of opposition between *talk* and *silence* is not as conventional as *hot-cold* or *big-small,* but it is recognizable and complementary; where there is no talk, there is silence and vice versa. The emerging paradigm here, then, of talking being honest, is now given a twist with the possibility that the silence being described here is not the companionable silence of people comfortable with each other, but lines up rather with the opposite of honest; *dishonest* or *deceitful.*

The opening of the second stanza also makes a contrast between the generalization of the first stanza and the specificities of the second. While the statement of what ought to be is aimed at the universal, the statement of what is not is focused on the narrator and his presumed partner. The focusing in on the particular bed and the specific relationship is given more emphasis by the next line, which begins *Outside* . . . and thereby constructs the *inside* of the room by implication. The reader may expect there to be some kind of contrast as the narrator seems to escape the stultifying silence of the bedroom, but in fact what we get is an almost Gothic reflection in the weather of the torment that is playing out in the bed:

> the wind's incomplete unrest
> Builds and disperses clouds about the sky

The use of a double negative to describe the wind here may prompt the reader to consider the need for a cumbersome structure of this kind. The wind is presumably not settled into a predictable pattern, (*unrest*), and yet there may be periods when the turmoil is quieter for a while (*incomplete*). Echoing the tossing and turning in the bed, perhaps with periods of sleep or at least apparent calm, the double negative emphasizes the fact that any periods of stillness are deceptive, since the *incomplete unrest* can clearly not be equated to *complete rest,* as many pedants might wish to argue.

The other opposition that Larkin exploits in this stanza is the lexically unconventional, but recognizable distinction between *builds* and *disperses,* which is a directional opposite, whereby one activity reverses the process and effect of the other. Directional opposites take place in time, of course, and this opposite, therefore, allows the reader to 'see', like a speeded-up film, the various moods that come upon the silent, brooding couple and then periodically dissipate, echoed in the clouds that they may be looking up at through the window.

Line 8 introduces the implied first person narrator for the first time, in the plural pronoun, *us.* It is implicitly contrasted with the rest of the world, by the phrase *None of this,* which refers back to the clouds, the wind and the *dark towns.* The natural world, and the world of people, then, are collectively referred to in this phrase, and shown to be at odds with the referents of the pronoun *us* by not caring for them. The implied conventional opposition in this juxtaposition, then, is *them* and *us,* which would normally suggest that the referents of *us* were united; in this case, united, it seems, in their misery.

The next sentence asks a question which takes us through to the end of the poem, and sets the scene by defining the two people in bed as being *At this unique distance from isolation.* The implication here appears to be that being in bed with one other person is about as far as you can get from being alone. It is constructed as a gradable opposite, then, since there are presumably other distances from isolation that occur when you are with other people in different numbers and settings. These people, however, are at the extreme end, away from isolation, and yet they are not managing, as we have seen, to communicate.

The final stanza, then, gets to the crux of the matter, asking why it is *still more difficult* to find words that are both *true* and *kind.* The presupposition triggered by the iterative adverb *still* is that it has been difficult to do so in the past, and this gives the reader a sense that this relationship is not newly stale, but has perhaps been going wrong for a while. The introduction of *difficult,* also adds to the oppositional architecture of the poem, as it echoes by opposition the use of *easiest* in the first line. Thus, we have finally got to the heart of what it is that is actually happening, as opposed to the ideal that is represented in the first stanza by the deontic *ought.*

The adjectives *true* and *kind* each belongs in a conventional lexical sense relation of opposition, with *untrue* and *unkind* respectively. The requirement that the words spoken in bed should be both *at once*, implies that this is not normally to be expected, and that it is easier to be kind if you are untruthful, and probably easier to be truthful if you don't mind being unkind. Note that the normal usage of these oppositions seems to be as complementaries, with the logical relationship being that if something is 'not true', then it is *untrue*, and something that is 'not untrue' being *true.* Less obviously, but also normally, the opposition between *kind* and *unkind*, though evidently gradable in experiential terms, is often treated as complementary too. Thus, parents admonishing their children ('that wasn't very kind') will suggest that they should be *kind* to other children, when what they may really mean is minimally *not unkind.*

The last line of the poem depends upon, and yet challenges, the normal expectations that readers may have of these two related oppositions, by suggesting that if the lovers in their silent bed cannot find something nice (*true* and *kind*) to say to each other, the least they might be able to do is say something that is *not untrue* and *not unkind*. Here, the effect is achieved by the use of *or* to create a textual opposition between the two positives and the two double negatives. Since the last line would be entirely redundant if *true* and *not untrue* meant the same and *kind* and *not unkind* were also equivalent in meaning, the disjunctive structure indicates that we are to look for differences between these sets. The reader is therefore led by the pair of double negatives to change his/her perception of the sub-category of opposition from complementary to gradable; if something is *not untrue/unkind*, that doesn't necessarily make it *true/kind*. There is, in other words, something less than perfection in both of these scales (truth and kindness) and that is the more realistic expectation that we might have of a relationship with another human being. However, in this case, of course, we are aware that the beginning of the sentence is phrased more like a question than a statement, and it not only presupposes that there have been problems in the past (*still more*), but implies too that the narrator is having difficulty in finding anything to say that wouldn't either be a lie (and thus possibly kind) or be extremely unkind (and thus be true).

This poem, then, makes it clear that contrary to linguistic codified meanings and regular tendencies (a negated opposition normally implies that it is a mutually exclusive opposite), these two positive human attributes, truth and kindness, are neither present nor absent, but in a stale relationship like the one he describes, the best one might hope for is to refrain from lying and being unkind, while not being exactly true or kind either. This raises the question of what our established (coded, social) oppositions are, questions them, and tries to put them into a different category of opposition to the one we might automatically assume.

What does this imply for our understanding of how language/texts work(s)? To me it suggests the following:

- That conceptual categories are conventional – and to some extent linguistically based – rather than absolute or given.

- That they can therefore change (not being absolute or 'given')
- That we require some kind of framework (e.g. the 'idea' of complementary versus gradable oppositions) to understand them when they change.

These three statements are really three ways of saying the same thing; which is: language is a partially stable system or code which depends for its success on both the fact that it is coded, and the fact that this code is only partially stable. If you lost either one of these aspects of human language, it would not function. A completely stable system would soon lose its ability to relate to a world that is constantly changing. It would certainly not allow for communication between groups of people who had only just encountered each other, since they would have no way to 'enter' a system that was completely different and cut off from their own.

On the other hand, the kind of loose federation of slippery meanings and unstable structures that some seem to propose when they claim that meaning is continually and only dependent on all aspects of context would not work either. Unless a hearer has some kind of similar understanding of the words and structures (and intonation etc.) s/he's hearing, s/he will have no point of reference in order to understand the text. This is not the same as saying that textual meaning is all in the text – or all in the author's intention.

Perhaps more importantly, this analysis demonstrates that opposition is a linguistic feature that ought to rank alongside metaphor, transitivity and modality as a prime constructor of the semantic architecture of a text. Paradoxically, it is just that knowledge that readers have of the conventions of opposition in English that enable them to understand the significance of the ways in which poets and other creative writers often try to break down and challenge the conventional oppositions and opposition sub-categorizations.

3.4 Novel openings[1]

The study of oppositions in poetry having established that the creation of unconventional opposites is a relatively common feature of contemporary poems, it was natural to wonder whether prose literary works also tended to create oppositional meaning. Since studying whole novels or even short stories was unrealistic, given the qualitative nature of the analysis at this stage, I decided to analyse the openings of one hundred novels, from a wide range of genres and styles, including children's and adult's books and both popular and more serious literary works.

As the findings below will demonstrate, there is currently no obvious way to quantify the kinds of phenomena that I am concerned with here.[2] The result is that this study enables me to make a series of observations about the type, nature and effect of opposition-creation in the openings of novels, illustrated from among the hundred books studied, but with no numerical data to demonstrate the extent of the phenomenon more generally.

Another consequence (and/or cause) of the qualitative nature of the study described here is that the definition of the 'opening' of a novel was left reasonably fluid. Some novels begin more than half way down a rather small page, and others start with a full page of dense text. For some, the opening might be the whole of a rather short chapter, while others would have long opening chapters where the first page produces significant amounts of data. A quantitative study would, of course, need to choose an arbitrary figure, such as the first 2,000 words, for its scope, though this strategy could produce problems of its own because the data thus produced might not be comparable in terms of its function in the novel.

Here, then, I will report on the observations that were made on the data collected, which allows us to assess the range of possible functions of opposition-creation in different kinds of text and compare this text-type with the poems on the one hand and the non-literary texts on the other.

One striking observation of this data was that some novelists do not appear to set up their narratives using created opposites at all. Ian McEwan, for example, does not seem to use this technique in the openings of his novels or short stories.[3] One can only hypothesize in his case that the stories which will unfold in his work are unlikely to be reducible to simple binaries and that he might be characterized as a writer whose characters and their actions are not amenable to straightforward evaluative (good-bad) judgements. Other writers who seem to spurn the textual creation of opposition include Stephen King, whose adult horror fiction in the three examples consulted[4] do not seem to produce any new opposites either. In King's case, the explanation is possibly twofold. On the one hand, his novels are, unlike McEwan's, very clearly based on the conventional opposition between good and evil, and this may mean that there is no need to set up particular versions of this universal opposition in the first pages. Indeed, it may be part of his appeal that the reader knows to expect the standard opposition to emerge, but it takes some time to work out which is which. On the other hand, this study also produced the observation that narrative passages, much more than dialogue, are likely to produce unconventional opposition, and King's novels are dominated by dialogue, which is a more mundane explanation for his lack of use of them. The question of why it should be that dialogue would produce fewer created opposites is one that I cannot address here. It would need a study of opposition-creation in conversational data to establish whether this is a technique that speakers use on an everyday basis, though my general suspicion is that they do. So, hypothesizing that it is the attempt to reflect realistic conversation that stops authors using unconventional opposites in dialogue, may not be upheld by such a study. The other possible explanation is that it is the narrative where the values and ideologies of a text are located, and the setting up of any unconventional binaries that are fundamental to the plot would be likely to take place in narrative sections more than in dialogue.

Perhaps not surprisingly, those children's books which were included in the sample did seem to set up unconventional oppositions in their early pages, though these are often reducible in fact to the good and the bad. Two noteworthy examples are the Dr Seuss books, and in particular *The Grinch Who Stole Christmas* and the Harry Potter books, most clearly in the opening of the initial book in the series (*Harry Potter and the Philosopher's Stone*). In both cases, there is a division between two sets of people, and the focus of the story is on the side of one of these sets of people. The Dr Seuss story divides the world up into those people who love Christmas and those who hate it, and the Grinch as representative of the latter, is the 'baddy'. In the case of Harry Potter, the division is between those who are *magic* and the others, who Rowling calls *muggle*. In the opening of the whole series, the specifics of this opposition are not immediately addressed, though the magic/non-magic distinction is hinted at through negation in the first paragraph when the Dursley family is introduced:

> They were the last people you'd expect to be involved in anything strange or mysterious (Rowling 1997:1)

Before the reader is fully introduced to the *magic/muggle* distinction, these hints at a division build up, with the Dursley family on one side of the equation, though some kind of scale or gradable antonymy seems to be set up here:

> Mrs Dursley pretended she didn't have a sister, because her sister and her good-for-nothing husband were as unDursleyish as it was possible to be. (Rowling 1997:1)

Note that the trigger of unconventional antonymy (from Dursleyish to unDursleyish) is negation, as we saw in Chapter Two, but here it is a morphological prefix which creates the negation, and this in a sense makes the created opposition seem on the one hand foregrounded[5] by its oddness, as it involves a created word, and on the other verging on the conventional or acceptable, as anything that is built into the lexical items themselves appears to be embedded well within the language. The additional effect of the capital D in a medial position emphasizes the unusual nature of this item, and is clearly part of the indication that this word belongs to the Dursley family themselves, an effect which is underlined by the use of evaluative phrases like *good-for-nothing* and conversational hyperbole like *as it was possible to be*, which both indicate that this is in fact free indirect style (FIS).[6] So, the whole of the Harry Potter collection of books begins with an opposition between the Dursleys and their relatives (Harry's mother and her husband) and is seen initially from the point of view of the Dursley family, though the FIS probably already hints that the reader will not be encouraged to be sympathetic to their viewpoint. This textually created opposition is developed quite quickly into the one that is threaded through the novels, between the *magic* and the *muggles,* though the former are not all seen as good, and the latter are not all as bad as the Dursleys.

Though some novelists writing for adults, then, do not seem to use constructed opposition, and children's books, on a small sample seem to use them as a way of building upon universal opposites (good/evil), there are some novelists who seem to use such strategies in the openings of just some of their works. For example in the case of both Patricia Cornwell and Tony Parsons, one out of three novels by each author which was scrutinized was found to use constructed opposition in its opening pages. Parsons' autobiographical trilogy, *Man and Boy, Man and Wife* and *One for my Baby* uses opposites in the titles of the first two, but not in their opening pages. These titles play on well-known phrases which sum up the lifespan of a man in the first case and marriage in the second. Although conventional in the sense that they are familiar to English speakers, they both draw on more than one conventional opposition, the second one in particular being an ideologically loaded use of the complementary term for the male (man) and the converse term for the female (wife). This reflects nothing more than the 'traditional' and probably still widespread tendency to see men as independent and women as primarily defined by their relationships to men. The converse, of course, is the opposition that has a mutual dependency between the terms of the sense relation.

The third of the novels, on the other hand, has no opposite in the title, but constructs a series of opposites on its opening page, when the advice of a man that has not yet been introduced to the reader is recalled by the narrator:

'You must eat the cold porridge,' he told me once.

It's a Chinese expression. Cantonese, I guess, because **although he carried an old-fashioned blue British passport and was happy to call himself an Englishman, he was born in Hong Kong and sometimes you could tell that all the important things he believed in were formed long ago and far away.** Like the importance of eating cold porridge . . .

That's how you get good at something, he told me. That's how you get good at anything. You eat the cold porridge.

You work at it when the others are playing. You work at it when the others are watching television. You work at it when the others are sleeping. (Parsons 2001:3)

The two highlighted passages in this extract demonstrate two kinds of opposition trigger in action. The first uses a concessive construction (although X, Y) to show that what is expected to be a complementary opposite, the difference between Englishness and Oriental culture, in fact coincide in the man being referred to. Like the poets, then, this prose writer apparently uses opposition-creation in order to undermine naturalized ideologies of difference. Note, however, that there is a very strong deictic centre being set up here, with the Englishness being constructed by implication as *here and now,* by the auto-evocative use of *long ago and far away* to refer to his childhood in Hong Kong. These fairy tale kinds of references to the Orient, then, are not exceptionally challenging to the naturalized norms of Anglo-centric culture and indeed even the challenge to the West-East dichotomy set up by the concessive trigger is within the norms of colonial discourse, with the hybrid English-other being a familiar stereotype of colonialist ideology.[7]

The second highlighted section uses parallel structures and conventional opposites to create a paradigm of different opposites to *work*. The parallel structure frame, *You work at it while the others are Xing,* has *play* in the first case, which is conventionally opposed to *work* and then *play* is replaced by *watching television* and *sleeping* in the second and third cases. The new opposites are likely to be interpreted as complementaries on analogy with the *work-play* complementary opposite, and also because there is another complementary opposite (*you/the others*) which is being set up here too. Though the more conventional opposition for the second person pronoun, *you,* would be *me* or *I,* there is also a commonly evoked opposition between *them* and *us.* Here, the use of *you* and *others* invokes this competitive opposition, whereby the narrator (*you*) is advised that he can get ahead while his competitors (*others*) are busy with more trivial or unproductive occupations.

As with the Parsons extracts, there is little of interest relating to opposition in two of the Cornwell novel openings,[8] but in *The Final*

Precinct there are a number of oppositions of an unconventional nature. The main focus of division in the text is that between normality and abnormality. Only one half of this opposition (*abnormal*) is present in the text, so that the conventional opposition is being referred to by auto-evocation through the negative morphological marker in the prefix *ab-*. Although this opposition is conventional, as is always the case with auto-evocation, two new oppositions are constructed in the vicinity of this opposition and these have a complicated relationship to the normal/abnormal opposition which is setting up the problem the narrative will have to solve. Here are the opening paragraphs:

> The cold dusk gives up its bruised color to complete darkness, and I am grateful that the draperies in my bedroom are heavy enough to absorb even the faintest hint of my silhouette as I move about packing my bags. Life could not be **more abnormal** than it is right now.
>
> 'I want a drink,' I announce as I open a dresser drawer. 'I want to build a fire and have a drink and make pasta. Yellow and green broad noodles, sweet peppers, sausage. Le papparedelle del cantunzein. I've always wanted to take a sabbatical, go to **Italy,** learn Italian, really learn it. Speak it. Not just know the names of food. Or maybe France. I will go to **France.** Maybe I'll go there right this minute,' I add with **a double edge of helplessness and rage.** 'I could live in Paris. Easily.' It is my way of rejecting **Virginia** and everybody in it. (Cornwell 2001:1)

Though normal/abnormal is flagged up in the first paragraph, it is also clearly constructed as a gradable antonym, using the comparative more, so that we are made aware that this is not just not normal, it is as far from the pole of normality as possible. This usage is not dramatically unusual, but it does point out a problem with the categorization of even conventional opposites out of context. Opposites constructed by positive/negative forms like normal/abnormal tend to be seen as complementary, since the negated propositions that relate them are logically related. Thus, if something is not normal, it is abnormal and vice versa. This is not normally the case with gradable antonyms such as *big* and *small*. However, it is clear that in actuality there are degrees of normality so that it is not entirely surprising to find abnormal used with an adverb of degree (more).

What is more inventive, and thus relevant to the topic of opposition-creation, is the discoursal construction of a complex set of normal and abnormal referents in the rest of this extract. Thus, we first of all encounter the 'normality' of the wished-for drink and pasta meal, which is quickly followed by the relative abnormality of not just eating Italian (and knowing the names of the food) but actually being in Italy and really speaking Italian. The abnormality of Italy is then replaced by that of France, which then becomes a kind of imagined normality where the assertiveness of the relatively strong epistemic modal statement *I could live in Paris* is undermined by a modal afterthought *Easily* where the intention of strengthening the modality actually has the opposite effect. So, the normality of living in Virginia, which has apparently become abnormal is replaced in the narrator's imagination by the abnormality of living in Italy – or Paris – and then this latter becomes an imagined normality. Intertwined with this question of place, which is not dissimilar to the here/there complexity of Duffy's exploration of place and identity examined in Section 3.2, there is another created opposition, which is triggered by an explicit mention of its opposite nature and a conjunction: *double edge of helplessness and rage*. This is not conventional, since *helplessness* is, if not linguistically, at least conceptually opposed to *capability* or *control* whereas *rage* is opposed to *calm* or *contentment*.[9] The result of bringing the two together is that each takes on the features of the other's opposite. Thus, *helplessness* is configured as relatively calm (if powerless) whereas *rage* is implied to have some of the features of control – at least rage enables one to take action. In addition, the two conventional oppositions which are being combined here are presented not as gradable or as complementary, since they are co-present and thus more like a kind of perverse converse relationship where although rage normally moves one to action, in this case it is combined with a feeling of lack of control.

Other extracts examined also used conventional opposition as the foundation of unconventional opposites, and this is particularly demonstrated by the opening pages of Morrison's *Sula* and Rhys's *Wide Sargasso Sea*, both of which deal with issues of race, and in particular the oppression of black people by white people. We saw an example in Chapter One from *Sula*:

It is called the suburbs now, but when *black* people lived there it was called the Bottom. (Morrison 1982:1)

The construction of the names for the place where black and (by implication) white people live as *the Bottom* versus *the suburbs* is a combination of an auto-evoked conventional opposition between *black* and *white* and the names themselves creating a new opposition, though of course they are names for essentially the same geographical place.

Some of the authors investigated seem to favour the unconventional opposite as a way of setting up their stories in the first page or two. John Grisham, for example, uses such techniques in the three novels included in the data for this project.[10] Here is an extract from near the beginning of *The Brethren*:

> For the weekly docket the court jester wore his standard garb of well-used and deeply faded maroon pajamas and lavender terrycloth shoes with no socks. **He wasn't the only inmate who went about his daily business in his pajamas, but no one else dared wear lavender shoes.** His name was T. Karl, and he'd once owned banks in Boston.
>
> **The pajamas and shoes weren't nearly as troubling as the wig.** It parted in the middle and rolled in layers downward, over his ears, with tight curls coiling off into three directions, and fell heavily onto his shoulders . . . (Grisham 2000:1)

In introducing the eccentric character being described here, Grisham first of all describes his clothes (maroon pajamas and lavender terrycloth shoes) and in the next sentence sets these two items against each other by the use of the conjunction *but* (see first highlighted section). Note that what is being contrasted here is the rarity, and thus the extent of eccentricity, of the items concerned, so that the whole of each clause is contrasted by the commonplace nature of the pajamas as against the idiosyncratic and daring choice of the shoes. What happens in the next paragraph is that this apparent opposition is abandoned when the pajamas and shoes are constructed together in opposition to the wig (see second highlighted section) in a comparative structure (weren't nearly as troubling as) which constructs them as gradable antonyms, with less and more troubling as the terms of the opposition. Thus Grisham uses the techniques available for constructing oppositional meaning to build up an image of increasing eccentricity as the features that first appear ridiculous are set aside to reveal the most ridiculous of all: the wig.

This creation of oppositional meaning often occurs in the openings of novels over fairly long stretches of text, and sometimes in a repeated process which replaces one opposite by another in order to increase the emphasis on the distinction being built up. Though it is to be expected that created oppositions will also be found beyond the first pages of the books, the suggestion that one way of setting up the conditions for a story to be told is to construct some kind of oppositional relationship, which may be based on a conventional opposition but may not be, seems to be upheld by this study.

Not many generalizations can be made of course, given the qualitative nature of the study, but there do seem to be one or two tendencies which would benefit from more extended work. These include the observation that short stories (with the exception, of Joyce's *Dubliners*, which are reasonably long) do not tend to create unconventional opposites in their opening passages, and that narrative passages, rather than dialogue, seem to favour the practice of triggering created opposites.

3.5 Conclusion: The role(s) of unconventional opposites in literature

As will become clear in Chapter Four, and was already suggested in Chapter Two, the structural and semantic mechanisms for creating local textual opposites are the same, whether the text is literary or non-literary. However, the in-text effect of any single example of a textually created opposition is dependent on a range of local factors, including the genre and the topic as well as the individual preferences of the writers concerned. This is complicated further by any interpretative responses which may be invoked in the reader, depending on her/his background and experience, which means that there are at least three 'layers' to the constructing of oppositional meaning in texts. We will return to this complexity and the reception of it by readers and hearers in Chapter Five.

What the case studies in this chapter demonstrate is that there are certain tendencies in poetry and the openings of novels which may not be bound to genre, nor possibly limited to literature, but are nevertheless present in the literary works I have consulted.

Poetry, in the form of two collections by contemporary female poets, McGuckian and Duffy, and one poem by a twentieth-century male poet, Philip Larkin, has been shown to use the potential for creating opposites by a range of means, to challenge and alter conventional opposites by providing unconventional pairings or combining two conventional pairs in unusual ways and to challenge reader expectations about the nature of opposition generally by assigning conventional and unconventional opposites alike to surprising subclasses of opposition.

In the openings of novels studied, the potential for literary effect of creating opposites appears to be more oriented towards the plot of the narrative than in the poetry examined in Sections 3.2–3.4 so that in novels we see more indication in the created opposites of the main parties in any antagonism that will be at the root of the narrative. There is thus, at least in the hundred novels studied, less unconventional opposition created which challenges naturalized ideologies of how the world works, and more which set up the oppositions which will be relevant to the narrative to follow. Some (many?) of these are versions of the good/bad conventional opposition, particularly where the genre (children's literature, horror literature) produce such expectations.

The next chapter will investigate case studies of non-literary work, to examine the use of textually created opposition in such texts and compare it with the material in this chapter.

4

The role of opposition-construction in discourse meanings

4.1 Introduction – opposites in non-literary texts

This chapter takes case studies of different **text-types** (Stockwell 2002) and topics and demonstrates the breadth of the phenomenon of textual construction of opposites, though it cannot, by its nature, claim to be comprehensive. What each of these studies shows is that the local textual effect of an individually created opposite may have a much more generalized discourse meaning if it participates in either a series of such created opposites, or if it occurs in significant places in texts to afford the reader a view of the kind of world the writer is envisaging through the text.[1]

4.2 British General Election reporting

The first case study was carried out in 1997 just before Labour won power in Britain for the first time in eighteen years. I collected the national newspapers for the day of voting in this election (1st May) and from them extracted those articles and commentaries which were specifically related to the election itself. I then extracted all the examples where opposites were invoked or created, and investigated them to see whether there were any particular patterns in this data and whether these patterns were similar to, or different from, those found in the poetic texts I had studied previously.

In general, I found that there were a similar range of created opposites, using the same range of triggers and with similar relationships to the conventional oppositions of English. The following examples illustrate this range, with triggers of parallel structures and a negative construction respectively:

> Seen as quick-minded and smooth by some, unguided and smarmy by others (*Financial Times* Article)

> There is real enthusiasm for Labour. It's not just loathing for the Tories. (*Mirror* Article)

These examples demonstrate an issue of content in the reporting of British politics, which is the relentless interest it displays in judgements of good and bad in the characters of the main players (here, the former Conservative MP David Mellor) and also the general liking or hating of the parties in general, as in the second example above. The two-party system, and adversarial politics in general has generated a view of the political process in the electorate and in the press which reflects this binary division as a complementary, or mutually exclusive opposite. Thus, the very fact of liking one party, it seems, excludes the possibility of liking the other, and one is expected to either hate or love individual politicians too. Note that even when there is some acknowledgement that these emotions are gradable (*likes best*), the division of individual exemplars is again mutually exclusive:

> . . . let the professionals remember that the politicians that the public likes best are not the aloof ones but the human ones. (*Guardian* Editorial)

Here, the *Guardian*'s editor sets up two kinds of politicians; those that are *aloof* and those that are *human*. Although there is no simple correspondence between this distinction and the liking/hating pair that is also invoked, we are nevertheless led to infer that there are indeed only two kinds of politicians; those who separate themselves out from the rest of us and those who do not.

In party terms, this data confirmed that despite the existence of not only a third party and a number of other smaller parties, there are only really two 'sides' in this battle. The following example demonstrates this tendency in its use of the complementary pair, *win-lose,* and the lack of a third word to describe the antics of Paddy Ashdown, then leader of the Liberal Democrat Party:

> John Major is scrutinised for signs of a man who knows he is going to lose. Tony Blair is scrutinised for signs of a man who knows he is going to win.
>
> It was difficult to scrutinise Paddy Ashdown as he dashed around the last eight marginal constituencies of his campaign yesterday. (*Guardian* Commentary)

The tendency to use complementary (mutually exclusive) oppositions, whether created or not, in describing all aspects of the election are evident even where there might well be, conceptually at least, some interim positions or a gradable range:

> The 'evil genius' behind the strategy that has turned the party from unelectable to unstoppable in 10 years. (*Express* Article)
>
> But in the past two Parliaments, power that was merely on loan to politicians has been given away irredeemably to Brussels. (*Times* Editorial)
>
> . . . most people are not interested in the big constitutional questions but in bread-and-butter issues. (*Financial Times* Article)

These three examples, from quite different newspapers and on different topics, each mark out the two options, as they see it. Political parties are either *unelectable* or *unstoppable,* power is either *on loan* or *given away*; political issues are either *constitutional* or *bread-and-butter.* Though readers would quite readily work out that these are not necessarily the only options, there is a question, which I will return to, over whether the repetition of complementary types of opposite in this way reinforces an existing tendency to divide the world into two in this fashion.

Although the ubiquity of the complementary opposite was the most striking tendency in this data, there were two further patterns that are worthy of note here. One is the tendency for paradigms of opposites to be set up, as in the following example which indicates that even at this early stage in Labour's successful decade, there was also a rumbling of distrust about some of its practices:

> Blair may be the pretty, public face of New Labour. But to people like Clare Short, Mandelson is the sinister 'man in the dark' behind the Labour leader. (*Express* Article)

The constructed opposites here seem to line up in a paradigm of *public/Blair/good* on the one hand and *private/Mandelson/bad* on the other. These paradigms are partly conventional (*public/private* and *good/bad*) but are invoked by unconventional opposites *public/ dark, Blair/Mandelson* and *pretty/sinister.* While the quasi-universal opposition of *good* and *bad* seems to be behind this example, the normal gradability of this conventional opposition is backgrounded in favour of a more mutually dependent kind of relationship, almost as though one cannot exist without the other. This kind of co-existent opposition, which linguists would term converseness, would feed the sense that voters might have of political parties not being trustworthy, even when they seem to be superficially a force for good. A similar effect can be seen in the following extract:

> For the 1997 election campaign has been distinguished by two contradictory but intimately related phenomena. It has been the most tightly controlled and 'professional' campaign in living memory. And it has been the campaign which has given least satisfaction and involvement to the voters. (*Guardian* Editorial)

Here, there is an explicit trigger of the opposites (*contradictory*) and yet the editorial claims that the two terms of this created opposition are in some sense co-dependent. Thus, it is implied, although one might expect satisfaction in the electorate at a 'job well done' in the sense that the campaign was 'professional', paradoxically, the voters were dissatisfied as a result of this lack of involvement. This same complaint was also voiced by editorials in other major newspapers:

> Some people are worried that democracy is being tainted by the slick professionalism of modern campaigning . . . the whole business has been so packaged and controlled and pre-fixed and sound-bited that it's not real . . . American superficiality has finally destroyed our fine old hustings tradition. (*Independent* Editorial)

> There was a real battle in this election campaign, but it had not much to do with that between the parties. It was a struggle between packaging and content, between politicians as soap powder and parties as vehicles for informed debate. (*Financial Times* Editorial)

Interestingly, the oppositions created here revert to the more common type of complementary opposite, in the first case contrasting *real* with *superficiality,* and in the second case *packaging* and *content* or *politicians as soap powder* with *parties as vehicles for informed debate.* In both cases the contrast is portrayed as a battle, in the first case by the metaphor of the final sentence where *destroy* is the verb linking the two terms of the contrast, and in the second case with the reference to *a real battle* and *a struggle.* This, of course, is not exactly a new metaphor for political campaigning and could be analysed in the light of cognitive metaphor theory (see Lakoff and Johnson 1980; Lakoff 1993) which argues that the ubiquity of certain metaphorical tendencies in society and culture lead to a situation whereby there is a naturalized or automatic referencing of an underlying conceptual metaphor such as POLITICAL CAMPAIGNING IS A BATTLE. However, the focus here is on the detail of how even underlying conventional ideas such as this cognitive metaphor are played out in the local features of texts. In this example, the lining up of the conventional metaphor of political parties being two sides in a war with the two aspects of another relatively familiar opposition, that between form (packaging) and content lends both conventional oppositions a new angle.

Although the reporting of the 1997 election did seem to favour the setting up of more complementary opposites, there was also some discussion about the nature of opposition itself, and in particular its foundational dependence on similarity. The following, for example, picks up Tony Blair's use of an apparently contradictory phrase:

> The 'radical centre' is the verbal ground where he has finally located the party. He insists it is not an oxymoron. . . . For the centre was the only place you could build a consensus. How, then, could it be truly radical? (*Guardian* Blair interview)

The question of whether *radical* and *centre* are contradictory is explored, and Blair's assertion that they are not is mildly countered in the last sentence of this extract. However, it is noticeable that behind this debate is the shared assumption on both sides that these two are the only options, thus confirming a recent development away from the three-term set of *left-centre-right* that was evident in earlier discussion of political ground. What would seem to be happening, despite the semantics of the word *centre* itself, is that the two extremes of *left* and *right* are categorized together, with the complementary term being the *centre*. Without further reader-response work the effects on popular perceptions of political allegiances can only be hypothesized, though it is likely at least to restrict the apparent options that are perceived from three to two.[2] Of course, the two main parties are both now generally considered by the press to be occupying the centre ground, so that the choice between two options of *radical* and *centre* looks increasingly like no choice at all, when the radical is often actually the extreme of reactionary in the 'old' terminology, with parties like UKIP (United Kingdom Independence Party) and the BNP (British National Party) vying for disaffected voters from both major parties, and the Green Party, the AGS (Alliance of Green Socialists) and other left-wing parties getting almost no press coverage at all. In such a situation, then, the commentary from the press is about similarity where there ought to be contrast:

> allowed the election to become a choice between the governing party telling the people 'you'll get sod all' and an Opposition saying 'sorry, you'll get sod all'. (*Guardian* Article)

Here, with the (almost) conventional oppositions between the *governing party* and *an Opposition*, and the explicit trigger of oppositeness, the phrase *a choice between*, the reader is primed to expect an opposition. In fact, what s/he gets is a minimally distinct parallel structure (*you'll get sod all*), where the lack of difference is highlighted by the addition of an apology (*sorry*) by the Opposition. This example illustrates the mechanism that I would suggest is in operation here:

- Readers interpret unconventionally paired words and phrases as opposites in the context of one or more of the standard 'triggers';

- The resulting unconventional opposites are understood in relation to specific conventional opposites and the general concept of oppositeness in the language spoken (possibly some of this a universal feature of human language);

- Where the triggers are in place, and yet no oppositeness occurs, as in the above example, the pragmatic effect is that the lack of an expected difference creates a conversational implicature which in this case is 'hard luck'.

In other words, with the contextual clues for the presence of opposition not being fulfilled, the reader is likely to conclude that an expected contrast is absent, and that this is the message of the utterance itself. This process of interpretation could be explained in Gricean terms (Grice 1975), as a flouting of the maxim of quantity, since the same information could have been delivered more simply with only one of the two parallel structures being used. The implicature thus produced will be that one might have expected a contrast here, but there is none.

A final pair of examples returns this case study to the discussion not of parties and movements, but of individuals. The following quotation from Peter Mandelson, widely reputed to have been the inspiration behind the New Labour project, is iconic of the contrast that it purports to be based on:

I'm not a manipulator, I'm a manager. (*Express* Article)

As we saw earlier in some poetic examples, alliteration is sometimes one of the triggers that link two prospective terms of an unconventional opposition. Here, Mandelson is trying to make a distinction between what he is often accused of (manipulating) and what he claims to be doing (managing). The iconicity arises in the fact of him actively manipulating the meanings of words, by choosing to use a different label to cover exactly the same range of activities. Note that he does not say 'I am not manipulating, I am managing', in which case he might be claiming to be doing different things, rather than simply labelling differently the same activities. Note also, that in drawing attention to these terms as candidates for opposition, he inevitably sets the reader thinking about the salient dimension along which these words might be opposed. In Mandelson's intention this may have been the dimension of meaning to do with interference; the manipulator interferes and the manager doesn't. It could be that for some readers, suffering under the burden of over-bureaucratic management, the term *manager* has altogether different connotations, likely to contrast with *manipulator* in a rather more negative way; in such a case, the reader may see *manipulator* as intervening (rather than interfering) and the manager as blindly following some set of bureaucratic rules – or imposing them.

The 1997 election data set shares with the poems the capacity to exploit our expectations of particular sub-categories of opposition. Here, for example, a comparative trigger is used to set up gradable oppositions:

> What kind of democratic mechanism can be found that is more than a nation-state but less than a federal government? (*Guardian* Comment)

Here, the difference between *nation-state* and *federal government*, which is normally assumed to be complementary (a state has to be one or the other), is being constructed instead as a gradable opposition by the use of *more . . . than . . .* and *less . . . than . . .* constructions. The changing between sub-categories of familiar (if not conventional) opposites is common in all the data, but in this data at least it seems to move more frequently in the direction of complementary opposition than towards gradability.

The 1997 election data set also produces examples of apparently incompatible, but co-occurring opposites:

> For the 1997 election campaign has been distinguished by *two contradictory but intimately related phenomena*. It has been

the most tightly controlled and 'professional' campaign in living memory. And it has been the campaign which has given least satisfaction and involvement to the voters. (*Guardian* Editorial)

This extract appears to claim that two supposedly mutually exclusive conditions co-existed at that time: the campaign was professional, but didn't appeal to voters. On closer inspection, this does not seem surprising, and the alleged correspondence between professionalism and voter satisfaction is only superficial anyway. This kind of journalistic 'play' with notions of opposition is common in political reporting, though it also obscures underlying assumptions about the nature of the world, behind apparently incisive, but actually quite trivial, debate.

One of the more common tendencies in exploiting sub-categories of opposite is the conversion of gradable antonyms to complementaries, as we can see in the following example from the 1997 election data:

The ballot paper may be marked *in enthusiasm, in fury or in resignation.* But the one emotion that should be absent for this one day is *indifference.* (*Times* Editorial)

Here, we have the positioning of three strong emotions (*enthusiasm, fury* and *resignation*), each normally at one end of their own gradable range, in a mutually exclusive opposition with *indifference,* which is the lack of any emotion. This neatly turns voter interest into a complementary opposition, with the strong implication that to feel any emotion strongly is an absolute good, and to be unconcerned about the result of the poll is absolutely bad. We will consider the potential social impact of such manipulations of sense relations in Chapter Five.

What we learn from the data in this case study is that the same kinds of meaning-construction appear to be used in political news reporting as in other text-types and genres, and the same general kinds of effect may be hypothesized. However, the nature of the data is such that the specific effects, particularly of repeatedly similar opposition-construction, such as the abundant use of complementaries, has a large potential impact on readers' views of political ideas generally.

4.3 Responses to 9/11

We saw earlier that some of the textually constructed opposites in poetry and news reporting had the tendency to both set up a mutually exclusive opposition and paradoxically also construct it as a co-occurring contrast at the same time. One of the more striking cases of textual opposition appearing to have a broader discourse meaning is to be found in the immediate reactions to the events of September 11th 2001, when the two hijacked planes were flown into the World Trade Center in New York and other planes were crashed into the Pentagon near Washington and Shanksville, Pennsylvania. In these texts, which respond particularly to the New York events, there was a concentration of such oxymoronic contrasts to be found.

In the immediate aftermath of the attacks, there was an unusual set of articles published in *The Guardian* which were journalistic in nature, but written by well-known creative writers. The articles in this small data set were:

- *Beyond Belief* by Ian McEwan (A: Wednesday 12th September 2001)

- *'We weren't there for Troy or the burning of Rome. This time there were cameras'* by Blake Morrison (Friday 14th September 2001)

- *Only love and then oblivion. Love was all they had to set against their murderers* by Ian McEwan (B: Saturday 15th September 2001)

- *Fear and Loathing by* Martin Amis (Tuesday 18th September 2001)

Although these are renowned writers of very different genres and styles of literature, there was a remarkable synergy in their responses to the events of September 11th, and although the data demonstrated a number of interesting stylistic features, one group of examples resonated particularly strongly with me as I was already working on textual construction of opposites in other data. This group of examples was spread across the work of these writers, all of whom have their own individual style. Nevertheless, they all repeatedly used a similar kind of semantic mechanism which created a mutually exclusive type of opposite and simultaneously presented the two terms of the opposite as co-occurrent in the events in New York. By presenting these paradoxical descriptions, the writers appeared to be trying to capture in words the unbelievability and unacceptability of what they knew to be true and what they witnessed with their own eyes.

In one case, the opposite is triggered by the change of state verb (Levinson 1983) *become*:

the *screen* became the only *reality* (McEwan A)

Here, we are presented with the ironic truth of people's experience that day; that what is normally considered to be unreal – the stories that we watch on television and film screens, was not only real itself, but took over from whatever was the reality of the individual lives of the viewers. The merging of ideas of reality and unreality is omnipresent in these responses, and the comparisons with filmic disasters are often explicit:

We had seen *this* before, with giant budgets and special effects, but *so badly rehearsed.* (McEwan A)

The implication of this contrast, triggered by the conjunction *but,* is that the truth of a genuine disaster is much more shocking than those that are created for Hollywood. Thus, we have a disaster playing out on the screen which is simultaneously familiar as a fictional genre because of the disaster movies that we know and also unfamiliar because of its reality and its extreme nature.

The other examples of oxymoronic contrasts being constructed in these responses fall into two groups in terms of their meaning. The first is a group of examples where the negative view of the violence and destruction of the attack on the twin towers is nevertheless qualified by a positively evaluated assessment of the thought and work that went into its execution:

A week after the attack, one is free to taste the bile of its *atrocious ingenuity.* (Amis)

If the *architect of this destruction* was Osama bin Laden, who is a qualified engineer, then he would certainly know something about the stress equations of the World Trade Centre. (Amis)

the Tuesday Terror, for all its *studious viciousness,* was a mere adumbration. (Amis)

The syntactic construction of these clashing oppositions varies. In the first case, the head noun is the positive term of the opposition (*ingenuity*) and it is premodified by a negative adjective (*atrocious*). In the second case, the terms are both nouns, and the positive (*architect*) is the head noun, while the negative (*destruction*) is in a postmodifying prepositional phrase. In the third case, the negative term (viciousness) is the head noun, and the positive term (*studious*) is a premodifying adjective. Despite these superficial differences, the examples seem to have more in common semantically than they lack syntactically. The sense of a world where the difference between good and bad or right and wrong has come crashing down is palpable in these admissions that the attack on the Twin Towers was on some level impressive. This sentiment is even clearer in the final group of examples from this data:

Even the flames and smoke were *opulently evil,* with their vampiric reds and blacks. (Amis)

The bringers of Tuesday's terror were morally 'barbaric', inexpiably so, but they brought a *demented sophistication* to their work. (Amis)

those towers collapsing with *malign majesty* (McEwan B)

the *majestic abjection* of that double surrender (Amis)

The first example is quite grudging, defining the smoke and flames as *evil,* though with a gesture towards something rich rather than paltry in the qualifier *opulently.* A similar grudging respect is shown in the second example, where the statement that the terrorists were *morally barbaric* is contrasted with the statement that *they brought a demented sophistication to their work.* This latter phrase, *demented sophistication,* appears to be self-contradictory. The whole point of sophistication, surely, being that it is under control, whereas *demented* indicates something completely out of control and lacking the civilized appearance of the sophisticated.

These two examples are in the same vein as, but outclassed by, the final pair of examples, where the use of *majesty/majestic* brings them into comparison. Though *malign majesty* has the positive term in head noun position with a negative modifier, and *majestic abjection* has the reverse structure, they both achieve the same kind of effect, by combining the awe-inspiring nature of the collapse of the towers with the terrible and distressing knowledge of how they came to be falling. The sense, then, of something that manages to impress while at the same time being one of the most awful events that people have ever witnessed is at the heart of this immediate reaction to the attack and is reflected in the writers' use of oxymorons of this kind.

What this case study seems to demonstrate is that there can be local meanings constructed in response to particular events and historical contexts which may be partly created by the repetitive use of certain oppositional structures, in this case oxymoronic ones, even where there are a number of different writers. This is the same kind of process that I postulated in Jeffries (2003), where a particular discourse definition of *water* seemed to be evident during the water crisis in Yorkshire.

4.4 The female body

In a study I carried out into the textual construction of women's bodies in women's magazines (Jeffries 2007), I found that one of the significant structuring devices used in the texts about bodies and body parts was the construction of unconventional opposites of the kind I am investigating here. What was most striking about this particular part of the study was the way in which the majority of the constructed opposites were related either explicitly or implicitly to the three superordinate conventional opposites: *normal/abnormal; natural/unnatural* and *good/bad*:

> The textual construction of contrast, or opposition, seems less clearly pedagogical or informative in nature, tied as it often is to the superordinate oppositions of *good-bad, normal-abnormal*

and *natural-unnatural.* The overwhelming presence of evaluative oppositions, both conventional (. . .) and unconventional (. . .) indicates a hugely normative drive in this data toward an ideal, youthful and unchanging body shape, irrespective of age or life's experiences. (Jeffries 2007:128)

Thus, the pregnancy texts highlight natural birth as an ideal that pregnant women aspire to:

> . . . says she hopes for a natural birth, 'though I'll probably start off with *whale music* and end up with *an epidural*!' (*Pregnancy and Birth*)

This example sets up *whale music* in opposition to *epidural* in the context of the conventionally opposite term, *natural.* While this may seem familiar to many readers, since recordings of whale music have, for some time, been marketed as a soothing accompaniment to labour, there is nevertheless nothing intrinsically natural about whale music in this setting in preference to the available drugs of any particular era, which just happen to be provided in epidural form in the 21st century. Though there may be many principled reasons for preferring less intervention in childbirth, the point is that there is no essentially 'natural' system of pain relief, and all attitudes to support in childbirth are at least partly cultural and socially constructed. However, the text in this case constructs an amusing unconventional opposite not to challenge pre-conceived ideas, but to preserve the status quo, which is that women are entitled to all their wacky ideas about childbirth, but when it comes down to it, the doctors know best.

Another issue that arises in relation to pregnancy and childbirth relates to the way in which the conventional opposites are used. In the following extract there is an implicature that leads to us concluding that the earlier birth and death of Jac was neither *normal* nor *healthy*:

> After losing her son, Jac, just six days after he was born prematurely due to severe pre-eclampsia. (. . .) She'd had two normal pregnancies and healthy children (*Woman*)

This implicature arises from the very strong sense that *normal* and *healthy* have of their opposites, even when these are not spelled out. The result is, perhaps, not particularly contentious in relation to the implied epithet *abnormal*, since one might hope that pre-eclampsia is a relatively rare occurrence, though the value judgement implicit in abnormal is hard to escape. However, the *unhealthy* tag is even odder in this context, since the meanings of this word are usually associated with lifestyle choices (e.g. *unhealthy diet* or *unhealthy conditions*) and are not normally connected tragedies such as infant mortality or the conditions that lead to it. The danger, of course, is that as in the common lifestyle collocations, an implication of responsibility will carry over into this context and the parent who suffers this kind of crisis will feel some sense of guilt. A similar potential problem arises in the following extract:

> The alpha-foetoprotein test (AFP) blood test is done between 15-18 weeks and measures the amount of AFP in the mother's blood. A high level shows an increased risk of spina bifida. A low level shows an increased risk of Down's syndrome. However, *healthy* babies can produce lower or higher levels of AFP. (*Pregnancy and Birth*)

While no parent – or even those affected – might *choose* to be afflicted with spina bifida, or Down's Syndrome, in the latter case in particular the implication that it is *unhealthy* is an odd one, and reflects current ideologies of perfection and bodily uniformity. These stark contrasts between what is desired (*good*) and everything else (*bad*) demonstrate a complementary tendency in this data which may encourage dissatisfaction in the readers and despair for those who are affected by such conditions.

The huge normalizing ideology that is observable in women's magazines extends to the detailed criticism of women who choose not to conform to current ideologies of the body, including pressure for women to have little or no body hair. In Jeffries (2007) I used the following extract to illustrate this naturalization of the pristine body:

> Nor am I the kind of guy who only goes for earthy types (you know, girls who prefer eco-terrorism to experiencing life and refuse to, like, shave and stuff). (*Jump*)

The article from which this was taken is allegedly written by a 19-year-old man who is attempting to argue that young girls should not dress too old for their age. In making his case, he uses the above extract as a way of convincing the reader that he is not an oddball, and he does so by juxtaposing the practice of *eco-terrorism* with *experiencing life*. The former, clearly identified as *bad* by the inclusion of the term *terrorism*, is also equated with not a *choice*, but a *refusal* to *shave and stuff*, which indicates the preferred norms of society in Britain at least.

The final point about this data from women's magazines is that some of the same kinds of opposite-construction are to be found here as were found in both news reporting and poetry. Thus, there are sometimes paradigms of opposites set up in relation to each other, as in the following extract:

> Remember, it's just as important to be *happy* as it is *healthy* . . .
> (Sugar)

What appears to be happening here is an amalgamation of two conventional pairs of opposites (*happy/unhappy* and *healthy/unhealthy*) and by this combination the two are equated. Thus, it is proposed by this text that the usual way that these two oppositions relate is that if you are to be *healthy,* you will expect to be *unhappy* (because you have to diet, exercise etc). However, the text is constructing the two oppositions not as related in this converse way (whereby the positive of one matches the negative of the other) but in a more benign way; that both are possible. While a positive message that may be uplifting in some readers' minds, there is also the normalizing drive towards perfection here too, so that the ideology of 'having it all' is clearly evident.

This ideology is never more present than in discussions of plastic surgery and other similar interventions. The following extract neatly exemplifies the kind of manipulation of conventional opposites that can occur:

> I had *silicone* put in so they're firmer than *normal tissue* but they still feel like part of my body. It doesn't feel like there's *anything* there at all. I think it feels very *natural*. (*Body Beautiful*)

Here, we have a constructed opposite of *silicone/normal tissue* which implies that silicone should be read as *abnormal tissue*. It is followed by the assertion that it doesn't feel like *anything* and this is equated to *natural* by the parallel structures *it feels___*. Thus, the most unnatural of interventions – the placing of implants inside women's breasts for purely cosmetic purposes, is constructed by this extract as simultaneously *abnormal* and yet thoroughly *natural*.

4.5 Those Danish cartoons

For much of this book, I have been concentrating on the effects and created meanings that occur locally in texts when two concepts are juxtaposed as opposites in an unconventional way. We have also seen (Section 4.4) that the repeated construction of certain kinds of opposition may contribute to longer-term social and political meanings, such as those constructing our perceptions of the female body as healthy/unhealthy, normal/abnormal etc.

In this final case study, I would like to take this idea of a discourse-level constructed meaning a little further, suggesting that the news media, in this case the daily national newspapers in Britain, may have an active part to play in the construction of certain rather significant meanings, often expressed in terms of opposition. In this case, as in others that I have investigated elsewhere, there is a meta-discussion by the commentators on the meanings of words and their relationship to each other, as well as some philosophical and moral statements that appear to be trying to set down the principles on which we may judge a difficult situation.

The kinds of emergent meanings I am concerned with here, may be quite local geographically and temporally, like the particular meaning of the word *water* that seemed to be emerging in 1995 in Yorkshire (see Jeffries 2003), though we may also note that these emergent meanings may reflect the zeitgeist too, or possibly influence a wider socio-political meaning emerging in broader communities of practice at the same time.

A similar process was noted in the meta-discussion of Tony Blair's 2006 apology for the invasion of Iraq, which is discussed in Jeffries

(2007b). In that case, what appeared to be happening was that journalists were driven to comment on Blair's apparent apology in a meta-discursive way, because the range of features that make up a speech act of apology, at least in British society, were not all present, or not all operating at the most prototypical way, in the case of the Blair apology. I argued there that one of the important features of an apology, as defined by these media commentators, is the question of whether it is accepted as such. In other words, the reader's interpretation of a text as a successful apology is one of the features that may influence the classification of that text as an apology. Other features included . . . This definition of the speech act of apology as a particular 'bundle' of sometimes variable features, may be seen in cognitive terms as what Lakoff (1982) has called a 'frame'. I will attempt in this section to apply a similar descriptive method to the current case study, which concerns not the meaning of a single word (*water*), nor the understanding of a speech act (apology), but the construction of a set of emergent meanings, including sense relations, relating to the phrase *free speech* and other lexemes in the same general semantic field.

In October 2005, a Danish newspaper published a set of cartoons depicting the prophet Mohammed, in response to a story that they had come across about the reluctance of artists to depict the prophet and put their names to their depictions. The newspaper had then run a competition for cartoonists willing to do just this, and had published a selection of the winning images. In February 2006, these cartoons became the focus of Muslim anger and there was a world-wide outcry, as well as further publications of the offending cartoons, debates about the issues of 'freedom of speech' versus 'incitement to hatred', and rallies and marches on both sides in many major cities. This representative example of the major problem facing the world seemed to be an event worth studying, as well as a likely source of constructed opposites (*Danish* versus *Islam?*) and I decided to collect news reporting of the crisis in British national papers.

The data collected for this case study was made up of all the articles found in the Pro-Quest newspaper database which contained the phrase *Danish cartoon** between 1st and 15th February 2006 and in the following papers:

The Daily Mail
The Daily Mirror

The Daily Telegraph
The Guardian
The Independent
The Sun
The Times

This small corpus was intended to include all the British national daily newspapers, though not the Sunday papers, which often have a summarizing function and have a tendency to repeat content from the daily editions. Unfortunately *The Daily Express* is not in Pro-Quest, and could not be found easily, so had to be excluded from this study.

The nature of news stories like this one is such that one could continue to collect mentions of them many months after the main reporting. After some experimentation, it became clear that this period (1st–15th February 2006) was the most important one for full coverage of the story, though even during this period there were a few which were minimally relevant, like one (ref?) where the footballer Michael Owen was said to have been 'treated like a Danish cartoonist'. The choice of *Danish cartoon** as the search phrase was relatively easy to decide upon, though I tried one or two other phrases, such as *Mohammed cartoon** and *cartoon** *crisis,* which confirmed my original choice as the more productive. The asterisk, of course, functions as a wild character, and allows for *cartoons, cartoonist(s)* etc.

The large majority of the articles (106 in all) were fully focused on the issue of the publication of the cartoons, although a few of them were only a short letter or were mainly concerned with other stories such as the treatment of Iraqi prisoners at Abu Ghraib prison.

Once the data was stored, each potential trigger for an opposite was marked and considered in context to establish whether there was in fact any kind of opposition being constructed there. In most cases there was, though sometimes, as we shall see, the difference between equivalence and opposition is minimal. In analysing the data, it soon became apparent that, unlike in the data relating to the female body, I was not finding the naturalization of a single accumulated ideology relating to this particular story. More like the discussion of Tony Blair's apology, there seemed to be a range of opinions and contributions to the debate, though they did fall into two different approximate groupings; those which were constructing the concept of free speech in opposition to incitement to hatred, and those which were doing something more subtle than this.

Nevertheless, I attempted to organize the kinds of meaning that I had found into patterns, even if they were contradictory ones or from different viewpoints (should publish/shouldn't publish etc.). This emergent meaning method (see also Jeffries 2003), argues that the actual meanings of texts are dependent not only on the codified language structures and forms, and the contextual features of the producer, recipient, etc., but are also locally produced in bodies (corpora) of texts produced close to each other in time – and probably in space too. The current corpus of data, then, presents a debate in the British press in February of 2006, about the freedom of speech issues raised by the publication of the Danish cartoons. It is argued that this crisis and the ensuing debate caused certain meanings to be constructed and began to be naturalized, though the patterning was arguably more diverse than in the case of the water crisis in Yorkshire.

The first thing that was evident in the examples of opposites was that the term *free speech* and/or *freedom of speech* was set in opposition to a number of different, but related terms, such as: *Muslim; intolerance of free speech; religious sensitivity; fatwa against Salman Rushdie; taboos in Islam.* Here we will consider just two of many examples of this kind:

> the issue had gone beyond a row between **Copenhagen** *and* **the Muslim world** and now centred on **Western free speech** *versus* **taboos in Islam.** (*Mirror* 3rd)

This example uses first the conjunction *and* to demonstrate the opposition between Denmark and Muslims (*Copenhagen* and *the Muslim world*) and then uses an explicit contrastive, *versus,* to demonstrate the larger opposition now in evidence, between *Western free speech* and *taboos in Islam.* Note that the occurrence of *Western* in the first part of this opposite implies that the second part may be interpreted as *Eastern,* though this word is not in evidence here.

Thus, we have some indication that the word *Islam* may be taken to include a semantic feature relating to its Eastern origin. This is not a necessary or historically consistent part of its meaning; as Muslims have spread through the world, the geographical link has weakened. Here, however, there seems to be a return to the simplicity of the East-West opposition which has been the focus of so many wars in the past. The other significant word in this constructed opposite is *taboos,* which could connote disapproval for some readers, as it may be linked to the irrational or superstitious. Thus, in what is on the face of it a neutral description of the problem that was arising over the Danish cartoons, there are strong hints of a particular viewpoint in this constructed opposition.

The second example uses a slightly unusual trigger, beginning with an explicit contrastive verb, *split,* in the first sentence and a pair of adverbs, *first* and *then,* to mark out the two sides of this particular opposition.

> The Irish are *split. First* there are **people like me,** who think that the Danish newspaper was right and brave to do it. *Then* there are **people like the President** who have so little confidence in the value of their own civilisation that they want to rush to assure semicivilised fundamentalists that they 'abhor' the publication of free comment in a free press. (*Mail* 14th)

The two terms of the opposite in this case turn out to be between the voice of reason and civilization and those who are apologists for *semicivilized fundamentalists,* such as the Irish president. Note that the parallel structures, including the postmodifying relative clauses, provide a further trigger for an oppositional interpretation as well as setting up *free speech* in a paradigm with *civilization, righteousness* and *bravery* as opposed to lack of civilization, extremism and lack of freedom.

Although the emphasis here is on constructed opposition, it is often difficult to ignore the relatively common examples of equating, which seem to function as a counter-balance to opposites in the texts, effectively providing a draft definition of the phrase *free speech* as seen by these commentators. Thus, *free speech* was variously defined in the data as equal to: *the ability to question* or *mock*; *the right to blasphemy*; *the freedom to ridicule religions* and *the right to offend.* The following are typical examples:

> Newspapers across Europe yesterday defended what one editor called the 'right to blasphemy' by printing Danish cartoons of the Prophet Mohammed . . . (*Telegraph* 2nd)

In this example, the phrase *'right to blasphemy'* puts *blasphemy* into the position where we might expect the phrase *free speech,* after *right to –*, and by doing so, equates the right to free speech with the right to offend. We shall see, later, that this is not always the case.

The second example of equating also involves the construction of opposites:

> The right of a newspaper to publish unfunny cartoons about Mohammed, Jesus or any other religious figure is *not* **a distraction in the defence of freedom from terror. It goes to the very heart of what must be defended.** (*Telegraph* 1st)

There is a contrast here between *a distraction in the defence of freedom from terror* and *It goes to the very heart of what must be defended* which is triggered by the negative, *not,* and which could be summarized at a higher level of abstraction[3] by pairs of words which are more conventionally opposed, like *central* and *peripheral* or *vital* and *unimportant.* In combination with this opposite, there is an important equating process happening, whereby the freedom of speech issue, here called *The right of a newspaper to publish unfunny cartoons about Mohammed, Jesus or any other religious figure,* is defined as being equivalent to the most vital or central value, which *must be defended.* Note that the opposite being constructed here is principally a gradable one, though the centre of a variable category is probably more absolute than the edges.

In some cases, the journalists argue that rather than being a fuzzy category of this kind, with a clear centre and increasingly unclear cases as you move outwards, there is instead an absolute sense of the phrase, logically more similar to complementaries than to gradable antonymy:

> Free speech (. . .) is an absolute in almost all instances, the safeguard of all other rights. The right to say only the right thing is not worth having, let alone fighting for. (*Times* 3rd)

> When it comes to freedom of speech the liberal left should not sacrifice its values one inch to those who seek censorship on religious grounds, whether US evangelists, Irish Catholics or Danish Muslims. (*Guardian* 4th)

> No one's religious convictions can be thought to trump the freedom that makes democracy possible. (*Guardian* 14th)

> The duty of government is not to pronounce on whether a particular statement was in bad taste, but to defend vigorously our fundamental freedoms. To do otherwise is to pander to a retreat from reason and free discourse as the foundations on which our prosperity, and our society, has been built. (*Times* 13th)

The following table summarizes the equating and contrasting effects of these examples:

free speech	equal to	opposite to
free speech	• an absolute • the safeguard of all other rights	• the right to say only the right thing
freedom of speech	• values of the liberal left	• censorship
the freedom	• that makes democracy possible	• religious convictions
free discourse	• our fundamental freedoms	• pander to a retreat from reason and free discourse

As we can see, when such equations and oppositions are presented in paradigmatic fashion, there is an emerging set of values here, which define free speech as an absolute good, with no shading or gradations. In opposition to this, we have a range of possible complementaries, including *censorship* and *religious convictions,* which could be interpreted as connotatively negative, and the more obviously negative *pander* and *retreat from reason and free discourse,* the latter being self-evidently good in Western democracies.

It seems, then, that such passages, which occur regularly in this data, are setting up a mutually exclusive opposition between the concept of free speech and the alternative, which is variously presented as intolerance and irrationality. We will see that this is not the only kind of opposition that is presented in the data under consideration here.

The other opposition which occurred repeatedly throughout the data was one which opposed secularism and Islam and often represented this distinction in terms that were tantamount to equating secularism with civilization and Islam with barbarism:

> France Soir published all 12 Danish cartoons and deplored what it called the new inquisition by 'backward bigots' in a Muslim world that knew little democracy. (*Times* 2nd)

The triggering mechanism here is more subtle than many examples, being reliant on the effective negator, *little,* so that it is made clear that *Muslim* and *backward bigots* were contrasted with *democracy,* which is taken for granted to be an absolute good.[4]

In addition to the complementary type of opposition, some of the commentators took the two terms of the opposition to be in a converse relationship, with each side dependent on the other for its existence. While this kind of mutual dependency is not necessarily a bad thing, and is usually exemplified in the literature on conventional opposition by the words *husband* and *wife,* there is nevertheless, the possibility that these two terms occupy the 'same' conceptual space, like an unhappy marriage, and that it is impossible, for example, to have free speech, without offence, or to have blasphemy without it being reliant on freedom of expression.

> We do not want to be deliberately provocative, but neither should we allow ourselves to be intimidated. (*Guardian* 4th)

This example, triggered by the conjunction *but,* manages to imply that the two terms of this created opposite, being *deliberately provocative* or allowing oneself *to be intimidated* are converse in meaning, so that if you manage not to be provocative, you are automatically being intimidated and if you defend yourself, this will be provocative. Nevertheless, the two negative triggers (not and neither) also hint that it is theoretically possible to avoid both courses of action, and this suggests that we might gain something from seeing the relationship not as one of mutual exclusivity but as a gradable range, with a middle ground being possible between offence and lack of freedom.

The other argument that is put forward against tolerance is the notion that this will have the capacity to undermine itself:

> He told us that our tolerant liberal society, which we had fought to establish over centuries, was in danger of being destroyed from within because that very tolerance meant we tolerated people who didn't share those same values and, as a result, they would undermine them. I have a horrible feeling that this is what is happening today. (*Independent* 13th)

In terms of the construction of meaning, what is being argued here is that there is a paradox at the heart of the word *tolerance* which, in its absolute form, would tolerate intolerance, and thus destroy itself from within. Although individuals may well be able to take a position of complete tolerance, then, a society cannot do so, as it is a logical impossibility.

Of course, Western (including British) society is not, in fact, tolerant to this extreme degree, as some of the commentators pointed out in relation to the legal restrictions on the freedom to deny the Holocaust in Austria and the lack of intervention by police in a demonstration in London where placards carried by Muslims carried slogans which were an incitement to murder:

> We can hardly exercise our political restraints to prevent Holocaust deniers and then start screaming about secularism when we find that Muslims object to our provocative and insulting image of the Prophet. (*Independent* 4th)

The hypocrisy arises, then, when societies claim extreme freedom of speech, but then impose some limits on that freedom.

One way that a society might deal with the offence caused by free speech is to apologize, though this is also a contentious area of debate:

> Why should the German government apologise? This is an expression of press freedom. (*Guardian* 4th)

Thus, the right to offend is sometimes supported in this data, though in the same article, the consequences of this right are also explored:

> The right to offend must come with at least one consequent right and one subsequent responsibility. If newspapers have the right to offend then surely their targets have the right to be offended. Moreover, if you are bold enough to knowingly offend a community then you should be bold enough to withstand the consequences, so long as that community expresses displeasure within the law. (*Guardian* 4th)

Thus there appear to be two opposites being created here; first a converse, that if there is an offender, there will be someone who can legitimately claim offence and secondly a sequential (possibly directional) opposite where the offence has a reaction which is legitimate if within the terms of the law.

Where the debate on this question in the press became more subtle, the uses and creating of opposites reflects this more complex response to the story:

> Publishing 12 indifferent cartoons a few weeks ago was justified. In today's climate, it is plainly wrong. (*Times* 3rd)

> The question has never been whether you draw a line under what is and what is not acceptable, but where you draw it. Rose and others clearly believe Muslims, by virtue of their religion, exist on the wrong side of the line. (*Guardian* 4th)

> It is a question of finding the crucial but shifting dividing line where free speech tips over into deliberate provocation, a line that changes with changing events. (*Times* 3rd)

These three examples demonstrate the attempts by commentators to reconcile the uncomfortable converse that is otherwise common throughout the coverage; namely the opposing of free speech and incitement to hatred as mutually dependent opposites. However, though there is some recognition that there is variability in either timing (in the first example) or the placing of the boundary between acceptability and unacceptability (the other examples), there is still a clear sense that there needs to be a division, even if it shifts. The final example above, particularly, echoes the traditional view that opposites, even when construed as being at different ends of the spectrum, may still have a clear point at which they become primary rather than a steady gradation between their properties. Note that this presentation of free speech and provocation is different from the one we saw earlier, where the two were converse, that is they were seen as co-existent and mutually dependent.

Rather like the apologies model (Jeffries 2007b), where there are a set of potential features of the apology speech act and sub-set of which may help to construe the speech as an apology, the conflict situation exemplified by the cartoons crisis and which typifies the free speech versus respect for others dilemma can be represented as made up of a series of features, some of which are gradable, and others of which may have a number of possible individual values. The main difference in this model from much of what actually happens in the data is that we would thereby identify 'free speech' as the name of the whole situation, and not one end of a spectrum.

The textual features of this bundle of features that I am naming 'free speech' include a range between the more subtle, coded ideational content and the plain-speaking extreme. An example of the latter follows:

> Here were Muslims carrying the Union Jack, denouncing the scumbags who gloat about terrorism, and making a peaceful and dignified protest about those stupid Scandinavian cartoons ridiculing the Prophet Mohammed. (*Mirror* 13th)

We may also include among the textual features of free speech the 'affect' value, as described in the following examples:

> They are not very *funny* (. . .) But they are certainly *offensive* (*Telegraph* 1st)

Is there, for instance, any non-Muslim who does not find the notion of the 76 virgins who await suicide bombers to be both *horrifying* and *amusing?* (*Telegraph* 1st)

Though there could be some debate about the textual basis of these emotional values and to what extent they are in the reader's reactions alone, there is no doubt that the commentators quoted here have made a judgement that the texts themselves encode such feelings.

The features of free speech relating to the producer include the authority or power to use this freedom, both generally and in relation to the recipient:

Conferring the same freedom of expression on more powerful organisations, including media organisations, is now less easily justified. Once we take account of the power of the media, we are not likely to think that they should enjoy unconditional freedom of expression. (*Guardian* 13th)

This feature, then, expresses the idea that one might defend freedom of speech more vigorously the more powerless the individual or group concerned.

Other producer features include the question of 'intention' – whether the text is intended to amuse, attack, explain, shock etc:

even if the intention was satirical rather than blasphemous (*Guardian* 4th)

Although offence might well be taken even where none is intended, the lack of intention might be seen as a mitigating factor. Here, however, the writer does not appear to accept such an argument. This feature might also be affected by the extent to which another feature, 'sincerity' (whether genuine or constructed) is in play and also by the awareness of the producer about the potential for effect on the audience or others, including by-standers.

The features of free speech which relate to the recipient are similar to those relating to the producer and include their authority or power (or lack of it) in general and in relation to the producer, the personal relevance of the text concerned and their levels of sensitivity to criticism/

attack, which may have been affected by personal experience or socially constructed sensitivity through folk knowledge and shared views. The following extract addresses some of these recipient issues:

> It is standardly said that free speech must include a right to say things that are offensive or provocative, but not rights to defame, insult, let alone intimidate. These supposed distinctions are inevitably unclear because interpretations of speech acts vary with audiences. Danes might read the cartoons as no more than *mildly provocative and offensive,* many Muslims have read them as *insulting and defamatory.* (*Guardian* 13th)

Note here that in addition to the textual construction of mild versus strong offence, there is also a supplementary opposite being set up between Danes and Muslims. This, surprisingly, implies that there are no people who may be described by both of these nouns and is reminiscent of, though less self-consciously ideological than, the Conservative Party poster that I began this book with.

As in the case of apologies (Jeffries 2007b), the recipient's reactions to a text will also partly determine the answer to the question of whether it is a case of free speech or a case of insulting. This notion that language is not merely harmless expression is captured in the following:

> Yet most speech acts are not merely expressive. They are intended to communicate, and may affect, even harm others. The nursery jingle 'sticks and stones may break my bones, but words can never hurt me' is palpably false. (*Guardian* 13th)

Other, situational features, such as the question of how public or private the text was, whether the text is directed towards those who might be offended or is actually intended for others, and the timing of the whole episode, including the response, are also relevant, but were less well-explored in the data for this study.

In summary, the 'Danish cartoons' incident and its ramifications in the British press have provided a case study that goes beyond a single text and demonstrates the negotiation of meaning, and in particular oppositional meaning, in relation to a specific news story and a very significant socio-political debate.

4.6 Conclusion: The role(s) of unconventional opposition in non-literary texts

This chapter has demonstrated that the creation of opposites in context occurs across a range of non-literary text-types and may contribute to a range of local textual meanings as a result. There is no clear dividing line between the created opposites in poetry and in news, since in both cases the construction of opposites in texts may be used either to challenge the status quo or to reinforce it. The socio-political implications, however, may differ indeed, so that the challenging of a conventional opposition in poetry would normally be a one-off experience for readers, whereas the creation of new oppositions in the news may reflect and reinforce conflicts of ideology repeatedly and eventually establish a naturalized new conventional opposition, such as that between Islam and the West, which was the product of George Bush's reaction to the attacks on the U.S. in 2001. Note that the creative writers who contributed to the immediate reactions to the events of 9/11 all challenged the mutually exclusive nature of relatively conventional opposites by creating clashing but co-occurring images. Their recourse to opposition as a way of summing up the feelings of those watching these events is just one of the pieces of evidence that demonstrate the importance of opposition as a generic concept in our society, even where it is changed or manipulated to bring us up against our own received ideas.

We will see in Chapter Five that there are potential explanations for the cognitive importance of opposition in our daily lives and communicative experiences. Here, I aimed to demonstrate that there seems to be some significance in the construction of new or altered oppositions in non-literary texts, and that these may have a range of potential interpretative effects, not least in allowing readers to construct possibly over-simplistic models of the complex world that they find themselves reading about in the news and other non-literary texts.

5

The significance of opposition in language and texts

This book began by trying to set the linguistic study of constructed opposites into a philosophical and psychological context, albeit rather briefly. I will conclude by putting the findings of what is primarily a stylistic study of a textual phenomenon into the context of linguistic theory, with particular emphasis on recent developments in cognitive linguistics as they have been taken up by stylistics, but not excluding equally important developments in lexical semantics, where opposites may appear, by rights, to belong. It is evident, I am sure, that there is still a great deal of work that can and should be done on this topic. The particular focus here on the textual construction of what would traditionally have been seen as a lexical semantic relation is only part of the picture. This chapter, then, considers the impact of textually constructed opposites on theories of language and speculates on how some of the contextual and cognitive theories of reader understanding might contribute to our understanding of the significance of opposition-construction in influencing the reader's perceptions.

5.1 A theory of opposites

One of the questions that the data in this study raises is what influence these examples of created opposites may have on an emerging theory of opposites. In answering the question 'What are conventional opposites?' prior to analysing this data, one may have answered with a fairly standard structuralist reply that they are pairs of lexemes with a stable semantic relation between them, encoded in the lexicon and having duplicate semantic components, with the exception of one semantic component, for which they will have maximally divergent values. This definition would reflect much of the thinking on opposition from the work of the Ancient Greek philosophers onwards, though the details of different sub-types of opposite are not considered by this formula.

If we take this definition very literally, we would have to include a number of pairs of words as opposites which would not be normally seen as being in this relation by native speakers. Murphy[1] makes a similar point when she distinguishes between two different kinds of opposite; canonical and non-canonical:

> The two types are not completely separable – their boundaries are fuzzy and it is not always possible to determine whether a pair is canonical or not. Certainly, *happy/sad* is canonical, but is *happy/unhappy*? If not, (. . .), then why does *happy/unhappy* seem like a 'better' antonym pair than *green/non-green* or *straight/unstraight*? *Wet/dry* is canonical, but is *humid/arid*? *Wet/dry* is certainly a more common pair, but cannot uncommon pairs belong to the canon? (Murphy 2003:10–11)

What Murphy seems to be doing is distinguishing between two kinds of opposite that are both defined in the same way, but where one kind is simply better-recognized as oppositional than the other:

> Some instances of relations, particularly examples of antonymy, seem to have special status, in that their relationships are well known in the culture and seemingly stable. For example, *hot/cold* seems like a better example of antonymy than, say, *steamy/frigid*, even

though both pairs indicate opposite extremes on the temperature scale. (Murphy 2003:10)

In addition to their lack of stigmatized status, the less common pairing is usually more specialized and less general than the common pairing. We therefore have a relationship of hyponymy between the two pairs in this extract, whereby *wet/dry* is superordinate to (because defined by fewer semantic components than) *humid/arid*. A similar relationship holds between another pair that I often use (see Jeffries 1998:103) to demonstrate the conventional (i.e. arbitrary) nature of accepted opposites: *tug/shove*, which are hyponyms of the conventional *pull/push*, but are not generally thought of as opposites.

Another step away from the conventional opposite, we might theoretically have pairs of words which also differ minimally along a single dimension of meaning, but which are not related by hyponymy to a conventional opposition. Every single pair of near-synonyms which might be described by an almost-matching set of semantic components would be candidates for this category. Thus, *stride* and *stroll*, two different kinds of walking, might in some analyses be defined by a minimally different set of semantic components, differing only in a feature that might be characterized as *purposeful/fast* in the case of *stride* and *relaxed/slow* in the case of *stroll*. Whatever the details of the analysis, these words would not be seen as opposites, unless the context triggered an opposite analysis, even if the minimal difference requirement were fulfilled. One might postulate that the reason they do not appear to be candidates for opposition is that they are not hyponyms of a more regular set of opposites, but instead are both hyponyms of *walk* itself, and thus are more closely associated with synonymy than antonymy.

Our first reaction to the idea that pairs of words sharing *even less* semantic denotation than this might be contextually constructed as opposites would probably be sceptical. If even near-synonyms, which are so close to opposites semantically, cannot always be construed as opposites, then why should lexemes which are 'complete strangers' to each other semantically be so? The answer, having looked at the data described in earlier chapters of this book, must be twofold. First, there seems to be a need for some kind of trigger, syntactic or semantic, in the context, to frame the otherwise under-related words as candidates for opposition. Secondly, whether or not there is a set of conventional opposites in the context, there must be one clear semantic component which can act as the dimension along which these novice opposites may contrast. Such a component will often, though not always, indicate a higher-level conventional opposition which may be seen as the superordinate opposite in this case. This, then, is a minimal version of the standard opposition definition. Instead of having a pair of words which is identical semantically except for one salient dimension, we find many cases in context of words being put into an oppositional frame, and by this process having their one potential for contrast highlighted for this occasion alone.

An explanation of the interpretation of textually created opposites in Gricean terms (Grice 1975) may help us to understand the possible interpretative process readers/hearers engage in when encountering a frame which seems to set up a pair of opposites:

She wanted a child. He craved a Cadillac.

The parallel structure in the two sentences of this invented utterance may set up an expectation that the grammatical objects are going to be opposites. This expectation is derived from the conventional opposition of the subjects (*she/he*) and the equivalence semantically of the verbs (*crave* is a stronger form of *wanting*). We therefore have two people who are opposites by gender both wanting something, but those things are not conventional opposites. A straightforward semantic reading of the utterance might not focus on the creation of a new opposition, and take the sentences at face value. However, many speakers would recognize that the parallel frames and the inclusion of gendered pronouns make another, pragmatic meaning also likely. This could be glossed as 'She wanted a warm rewarding relationship with another human being whereas he was obsessed by material goods'. There is, of course, a value judgement implicit in this gloss. Such a conversational implicature (Grice 1975) is a consequence of the under-specificity of the constructed opposite, in other words, a flouting of the maxim of quantity, where the reader is obliged to work out the semantic relations that are implied between elements in two parallel structures.

The explanation that could be given in Gricean terms could also focus on the expectation of a conventional opposite in the second object position. When that expectation is frustrated, the maxim of relation is apparently flouted, and the reader/hearer may carry out some inferencing work to establish in what sense these terms may indeed be interpreted as opposites, in order to preserve the co-operative status quo. At this point, the reader/hearer will draw upon her/his background knowledge about the way that oppositeness works by contrasting referents with similar semantics along a single, but stigmatized, dimension. The most significant differences, perhaps, between the referents of *child* and *Cadillac* are those relating to their animate/inanimate nature, and the value that derives from these; emotional on the one hand and monetary or status-oriented on the other.

So far, the explanation would have worked perfectly well had the parallel structures used identical verbs (e.g. *want* in both cases). The created oppositional context, however, will also highlight the difference in strength of the two verbs, adding a further inferencing possibility; that she only wanted a child (it's not much to ask is it?) while he spent *all the family budget* on cars. This inference arises from the difference in strength of the verb, and plays, therefore on both their semantic similarity and the dimension of difference (strength) that is highlighted in this oppositional context.

The question of whether – or to what extent – these inferencing processes involve reference to some kind of universal – or fundamental – opposites remains open. Certainly in the current case, I cannot see an obvious lexical opposition which underlies the usage, though one might recognize a conceptual opposition between material and emotional values.

This invented example highlights another aspect of the ideological loading of opposites that are constructed by texts. There could be a clear good-bad implication in the example I have just analysed, where the woman has the moral high-ground and the man is portrayed as materialistic and shallow, though the fact that these are pragmatic meanings would indicate that other contexts of situation may produce other value structures. I will return at the end of this chapter to the question of whether all or most of the constructed opposites we find have such value judgements attached.

5.2 Mental representations and schemata: The cognitive basis of opposites

What I have done in trying to place the unconventional opposites within the same model as the structuralist explanations of conventional opposites is to highlight the necessity of taking into account the reader's/hearer's role in interpreting these unconventional semantic relations. Clearly, a straightforward *langue-parole* distinction with rigid boundaries between the two would not explain how we see the novel kind of opposite in the same light as conventional pairs.

Perhaps the first place we could begin is by thinking about the possibility that opposites, of all kinds, have a mental representation for the speaker/hearer and that encountering a novel or unconventional opposite will both trigger the mental representation of a related conventional opposite and also lead to a new mental representation in the reader's mind. The notion of mental representations or 'mental spaces' derives from the work of Fauconnier (1985) who proposed that in talking (or reading) about the world, we conceptualize it in such a way that we have a fully worked model in our minds of the relationships between places, participants, etc. and can use linguistic expressions to develop these mental spaces, both in ourselves and in others.

Philosophical accounts of opposites, and lexical semantic accounts too, have emphasized the logical properties not just of the category of opposite in general, but also of the sub-categories as specified by different commentators. However, this logical view of such effects, in terms of the possible propositions, entailments etc. that a text might set up for the reader, have been set aside by those who are interested in how we understand opposites, as Murphy says:

> While paradigmatic semantic relations have been defined in logical terms (. . .) such relations reveal little about the roles of semantic relations in lexical memory and language use. (Murphy 2003:5)

A similar point is made by Lakoff (1982) in defining his concept of an ICM (idealized cognitive model) which drew on similar work by Fillmore on 'Frame semantics' (1982, 1985):

- They are structured wholes ('gestalts')

- They use natural (i.e. experiential) categories, not classical categories

- As well as propositional content, they may contain image-schemas

- They provide holistic frames for situations

In order to understand how such constructs may help us understand the basis of oppositeness, it is worth considering in a little more detail what is meant by image-schema. Here is one definition:

> Image-schemas (e.g. CONTAINER, PATH, FORCE) are pervasive skeletal patterns of a preconceptual nature which arise from everyday bodily and social experiences and which enable us to mentally structure perceptions and events (Johnson 1987; Lakoff 1987, 1989). Within Cognitive Linguistics, these recurrent non-propositional models are taken to unify the different sensory and motor experiences in which they manifest themselves in a direct way and, most significantly, they may be metaphorically projected from the realm of the physical to other more abstract domains. (Santibáñez 2002)

The way in which image-schemas have most frequently been used in linguistics, then, is to explain the basis of metaphor, but this is not their only possible use. What is significant about image-schemas, it seems, is their *preconceptual* nature. In other words, these are envisaged to be some of the most fundamental structuring mechanisms of human existence, since the implication in *preconceptual* is that they are philosophically speaking the axioms upon which the rest of human thought and speech is built. What Lakoff, Johnson and others do, then, is to take the notion of the image-schema as the building block and suggest that many of our common everyday metaphors (e.g. LIFE IS A JOURNEY) are constructed by taking a common physical experience (the journey) and relating it to a more abstract experience (life).

Some of the features of the ICM are potentially useful in my attempts to understand the cognitive basis of oppositeness and particularly of constructed oppositeness. Thus, we may find the logicians' view of the different logical potential of opposites interesting, but what we need to explain is the first language speaker's experience of and use of opposites themselves, however illogical that may turn out to be. It is possible that, like metaphor, oppositeness in all its complexity is built upon some natural categories which are also preconceptual because they are based on experience rather than conceptual processing. It is clear, for example, that the specifics of oppositeness linguistically have to be taught to children, albeit at a young age. What is not so clear is whether there is an experiential predisposition towards such contrastive ideas which makes it relatively easy to teach the specifics at such a young age. The classic Lacanian mirror stage of recognition of the ego, and thus of separation and differentiation from the 'other' may be postulated as one such possible source of the universal opposition.[2]

Emmott's (1997) work on narrative comprehension also builds on work in cognitive psychology on mental images and she claims that the online processing and interpretation of texts by readers cannot be explained by a logical or conceptual approach either:

> There has been particular dispute about the nature of mental representations. Propositional models have been criticized because they view each proposition as being interpreted in isolation rather than taking meaning from the reader's knowledge of the situation. Mental models, by contrast, provide information about the situation, having produced an image-like 'map' in memory. The research on mental models provides a useful base on which to hypothesize about text-specific representations, but needs to be supplemented by a study of the properties of real texts (Emmott 1997:72)

As Emmott points out, the work on mental models at that time was largely based on decontextualized and invented sentences, and her own work took the study of narrative comprehension forward by its focus on real texts and real readers. Although her interests are in the understanding of reference and reader comprehension over long passages, the study of contextually created opposites does, it seems to me, fit her notion of the kind of mental representation that would be needed by a reader in order to access the broader meaning of the surrounding text. Thus, in order to appreciate the particular viewpoint of the writer in the examples used in the preceding chapters, during online processing the reader would need to construct a mental representation which reflected the particular version of the world for the purposes of reading. In Emmott's model, this may form part of the *contextual frame* that the reader is seen as producing in real time in the reading process. The fact that opposites are sometimes created and then dismantled in the same text, of course, would support this view, since the reader is tasked with seeing the world in one (binary) form and then this viewpoint may be amended. The ideological implications of this mechanism will be discussed later.

Murphy's (2003) work is also cognitive, though it is not dealing with the axiomatic levels of image-schema that we considered earlier. However, like Emmott, Murphy emphasizes the need to see how the gap between our stable knowledge (of the language) and its use is bridged:

> The pragmatic and psycholinguistic perspective, then, is concerned with the relationships between competence and performance. Studying these relationships involves determining what one must know in order to know how to do something (like produce or interpret a meaningful utterance) and what we know as a result of having done this thing. (Murphy 2003:5)

She claims that we have four kinds of knowledge of language, the first three of which are needed to use language and the fourth being the kind of meta-awareness that is not needed except in order to comment on the language itself. These four kinds of knowledge are summarized here as:

1   fixed mental representations in long-term memory

2   procedural knowledge (rules)

3   generated mental representations

4   awareness

If we ignore the fourth kind here as irrelevant for our purposes, we are left with three kinds of knowledge that might play a part in the interpretation of novel opposites. If we take the three kinds of opposite that were identified in the previous section, it could be hypothesized that they are represented by the three kinds of knowledge. Thus, the conventional opposites would be established as lexical entries against the relevant lexical items in our long-term memory. The second kind of opposites, those which have all the usual characteristics except the conventional status (e.g. *humid/arid*), would be produced by general rule, and interpreted by the same process, on analogy with what is known (but not repeatedly processed) about opposites in general and the superordinate pair in particular. The third kind of opposite, those with which I have been mainly concerned in this book, would be generated as mental representations with a single strand of oppositeness foregrounded as the vital ingredient for their relationship in this one-off case.

If we accept this view of the knowledge required and used for producing and interpreting opposites, some of the consequences include the fact that, like strong collocational tendencies, speaker/hearers will be aware of the whole opposite pair where it is conventional, even if only one of the terms is actually used (I called this 'auto-evocation' in Chapter Two). This would help to explain the notion that when unconventional pairs of opposites include one part of a conventional pair, the whole conventional relationship seems to be evoked and the unconventional part of the new pairing is matched to the missing term. To illustrate this point, let us return to an example used in Chapter Three:

> Perhaps she purchased, by this biblical
> Applique, less a *genuine* daylight
> Than the *aplomb* of those winter-white insets
> On my edge-to-edge bolero. . . . (McGuckian 1994:21)

The case was made there that although *aplomb* would not normally be viewed as having an opposite, its juxtaposition here in contrast with *genuine* causes the conventional opposite of *genuine* (*falseness*) to be invoked as the significant characteristic of *aplomb* in this context.

Another consequence of explaining unconventional opposites in terms of the different levels of knowledge needed is that we must hypothesize different amounts of processing effort for the three different types, and indeed different amounts too for the variations on constructed opposite that were examined in Chapters Two, Three and Four. Thus, the closer the contextual opposite is to the prototypical relation and the more easily it can be matched to a conventional opposite, either through hyponymy or by partial mapping onto conventional opposites, the easier it must be to interpret. The most difficult case, it would follow, would be an unconventional opposite pair of which neither term is a member of another conventional pairing and where neither the context nor the semantics of the words involved provides an easy parallel with a superordinate opposite pair. In such cases, which are in the minority it seems, the amount of processing needed may well seem too much for the recipient who might give up in the face of the effort required. This is one frequent response to what is perceived to be 'difficult' poetry, where the construction of opposites is just one among many complicating factors which can alienate – or intrigue – the reader.

One way of approaching an explanation of how we interpret opposites in context is to call upon schema theory to help model the kinds of information we store and how we use it. Schema theory (see Schank and Abelson 1977; Eysenck and Keane 1990; Cook 1994; Semino 1995 and 1997; Jeffries 2001) is normally used to explain our cognitive storage of activity types and transactions between people. Thus we will have a schema for what is involved in buying clothes, ordering a meal, visiting the bank etc. and this will frame any actual experience of such events as well as being further modified by such experiences. We will, for example, have a script for what happens in restaurants which will include the processes by which a customer gets to sit at a table, how they order the meal and how it is paid for. This script may change as a person travels the world and experiences different styles of restaurant, and as the means of payment change through the years in response to technological innovation. There may also be unique experiences, such as having the soup spilled over you, or waiting excessively long for your food, which will alter the script temporarily. If such experiences happen repeatedly, they may have a permanent effect on the script. Although opposites are not social events in the same way, it seems to me that there may be some mileage in seeing conventional opposites (and possibly also other knowledge about language) as similar to schemata because they share some characteristics. So, for example, they too are acquired experientially, and can be called upon to interpret new opposites which we are not familiar with, but where we recognize some of the characteristics of oppositeness such as the usual range of contexts and the significant contrast along a single dimension of meaning.

The current work supports this view, in my opinion, by demonstrating time and again that the contextual interpretation of a certain kind of semantic relationship (opposition) is reliant on two kinds of prior knowledge on the part of the reader/listener. One the one hand, the conceptual apparatus for what constitutes a pair of opposites would be needed in order to interpret a new case. This would include, for example, the understanding that opposites tend to be actually quite close in meaning, but differ considerably on one salient dimension of meaning. The other kind of knowledge that would be required is specific knowledge of conventional opposites in the language being heard/read. While the precise list of what constitutes conventional opposites might not be easy to agree on, this may simply be because they form a prototype category rather than a watertight one. Thus, we may all find it easy to agree on a certain set of central, prototypical, opposites, (e.g. *hot/cold*) and less easy to agree as we get towards the edges of the category. However, it seems important, given the prevalence of constructed opposites in the data investigated here, that readers/hearers of language have reference points in their everyday competence, and the fact that many of the constructed opposites seem to be specific cases of the conventional ones would support the idea that we use our codified knowledge to interpret new meanings.

Schema theory does not itself make reference to the kinds of cognitive structuring that seem to arise from (or cause?) the existence of opposites, and yet it provides a useful way of describing the way in which opposites of various kinds might interact with each other since we recognize some of them readily, and are able to decode new opposites on analogy with these. Returning to the idea of image-schema discussed earlier, which is more fundamental than acquired schemata, one could even hypothesize that there is a generalized image-schema of opposition based on bodily experience (perhaps up/down or the me/other distinction discussed above), with no specifics attached, into which both conventional and unconventional oppositions fit. This latter notion would help to explain the apparent single category of opposites that speakers seem to perceive, even though there are very many different types of pairing subsumed into it. This explanation might help to mitigate the perplexity that Cruse (2004) among others expresses in the face of the category of opposites that appears to be ill-defined but is apparently clear to speakers. Davies (2008:79) discusses the problem in the following way:

> The assumption that there can be innate decontextualised oppositions may seem like common sense, but without further investigation into whether oppositeness is indeed an inherent natural or cognitive phenomenon – i.e. whether it exists objectively in the material world external to human thought or wired into the mind – it is difficult to substantiate categorically claims that oppositeness is inherent or patent. **'Up' / 'down'** do seem to be logically directionally opposed, as Cruse claims, but they are *relative* terms (as are **'hot'** / **'cold'**), in that their meaning still depends on the perspective of the person who uses them in discourse. Cruse is assuming that opposition *is* 'cognitively primitive' but does admit 'it is quite hard to pin down exactly what oppositeness consists of'. (2004:162)

An image-schema of opposite, then, could form the cognitive basis of a more specific but fuzzy category in practice which would be delineated by a set of variable features to be used to establish the prototypical member of the category, much like the mechanism used in Chapter Four to describe the variable features of the meaning of *freedom of speech,* and in Jeffries (2007a) to describe the features of the speech act of apologizing, but this time applied to a conceptually based linguistic category of opposition:

feature	range (more............less prototypical)
single dimension of difference	complementary......gradable...... converse/reversive
semantic similarity	all (but one) semantic components identical......none
conventional status	both terms......one term......neither term
syntactic trigger	multiple triggers......no triggers
semantic context	explicit contrast......conventional opposites in context......none

These features together delineate the scope of the most prototypical of uses of opposites in context, and only the first could be said to be a necessary feature, though in itself it is not sufficient, as we saw in the case of *stride* and *stroll,* two near-synonyms, but not opposites unless other factors are also in play. For each feature, the left-hand side of the range is closer to being prototypical, so that an example with multiple syntactic triggers (e.g. negation and parallelism) and having one of its terms drawn from a conventional opposite pairing will be more prototypical than an example with only one or no syntactic triggers and no term that belongs to a conventional opposite.

5.3 Conceptual metaphors, mental spaces and text worlds

Lakoff and Johnson (1980) are famous for having brought to broad academic notice the idea that much of our thinking, and particularly our abstract thinking as humans is metaphorical. This is now one of the basic tenets of much work in cognitive linguistics and has been the subject of a great deal of psycholinguistic experimentation (Gibbs and Steen 1995) including efforts to find out how readers decode or interpret novel metaphorical structures in literary texts (Steen 2002). I would like to make the case that if, as I suspect, opposition is at least as important a conceptual structuring device as metaphor, then an equal amount of attention and work needs to be expended on this topic. In the light of the data presented here and in particular the possibility that political opposite-creation is a force at work in our world, it seems likely that the power of the media, and politicians through the media, is hegemonic in nature and has the capacity to influence the world-view of many of the world's citizens. Given the apparent importance of some basic set of opposites in helping us to interpret novel opposites, we may even hypothesize that there are socially constructed and over-arching conceptual opposites (GOOD/ BAD) that will rank alongside the metaphor set (TIME IS MONEY etc.). What may be different, is the extent to which it is possible to create *truly* original opposites, though some of the examples in earlier chapters may qualify and some words (e.g. choice and freedom) seem to emerge as naturalized virtues at certain times. The range of possible models for interpreting a newly constructed pair might go from the default expectation that it is a complementary opposite to the less expected gradable, converse or reversive opposition. While we may 'enjoy' interpreting a novel metaphor, and may do so without recourse to a conventional or conceptual one – is this even conceivable for opposites, or do we absolutely need to 'translate' them into more familiar (more abstract) ones, such as *good-bad?* And to what extent are we able or likely to use a gradable or converse understanding of a new opposite rather than the more entrenched complementary?

The idea of 'mental spaces', mentioned earlier and first proposed by Fauconnier (1985) can help us here. He describes them in the following terms:

> Domains that we set up as we talk or listen, and that we structure with elements, roles, strategies and relations (Fauconnier 1985:1)

The important part of this description for my purposes is 'relations', which he proposes are added to the mental spaces that we create as we participate in linguistic communication, and which would be an appropriate description of the short-term relations that are set up in the context of constructed opposites. It is the temporary nature of these mental spaces, which might help us to understand the nature of the constructed unconventional opposite. While our experience of the world may lead us to create a set of relatively stable schemata about the way in which it works, which are then subject to amendment as our experiences demand, the daily interaction we have with others through written and spoken texts not only contributes to the stable system of understanding of the world but also creates a moving and temporary conceptual mapping (Fauconnier's domain) produced by the text as we move through it as producer or recipient. Emmott's (1997) conceptual frame is one possible result of this conceptual mapping, and another is the text world that Werth (1999) proposed as a development from Possible World Theory[3] (see Ryan 1991). Both Conceptual Frame Theory and Text World Theory grew out of an increasing interest among text linguistics in cognitive aspects of the process of reading. In both cases, the aim is to link features of the texts to the mental constructs which these theories hypothesize must be created during processing. In both cases too, it follows that the linguistic end of the link is defined in terms which arise from other linguistic theories and descriptive models. Thus, the various ways in which language references the world (actual or hypothetical), including deixis, modality, transitivity and nominalization among others, become the basis of defining how the 'world' produced by a text is constructed linguistically. What I would suggest in this context is that the textual triggering of opposition, conventional or unconventional, is another of the linguistic means by which text worlds are constructed.

The study of the openings of novels reported in Chapter Three gives us a small insight into this process. The opening of the first Harry Potter novel, for example, introduces the reader to a text world that is set up from the beginning as being made of two halves, the *magic* and the *muggle*. In other novels such a divided world may be progressively constructed as the characters reveal themselves. It would be difficult to read the Harry Potter novels without accepting this division as underlying the whole narrative, since many of the plots require this distinction in order to make sense. There is, of course, fiction where this doesn't happen, or where the constructions of opposites are more complex than the simple good-bad (e.g. *His Dark Materials* trilogy by Philip Pullman). Certain genres like detective fiction and 'superhero' films are predicated on the idea that the world is indeed divided into 'goodies and baddies', though in the former case the 'reveal' of which character is on which side happens much later than in the latter. In both cases, though, the world of the text has a very particular opposition that is presumably set up in the early stages of the narrative.

Not all world building, though, happens in the context of reading fictional texts, and not all of the binary divides that are constructed in texts are necessarily subsumed under the *good/bad* superordinate. However, we saw in Chapter Four that the world of women's magazines is constructed upon a set of repeated opposites such as *healthy/unhealthy*, *natural/unnatural* etc. and these do indeed line up under *good/bad*. Similarly, the news reporting of the Danish cartoons crisis had a number of *good-bad* opposites being set up. The responses to 9/11 are more complex, and the text world therefore which these texts set up is less clearly divided, since the oxymoronic clashing of these constructed opposites brings *good* and *bad* together in the shock of the early days of that disaster. It was perhaps not as surprising as we might think, since these texts were all written not by journalists but by novelists and poets, and their use of the constructed opposite was much more akin, therefore, to Duffy's and McGuckian's in asking questions about the established divisions in our society. In the case of the 9/11 responses, the actual world of the observer had changed so fundamentally that the use of the 'normal' range of epithets (*evil, monster* etc.) as used in run-of-the-mill crimes such as rape and individual murder, did not apparently offer the writers the form of expression they needed. The need to suggest that all the usual binaries of our world have come crashing down was clearly very strong as these different writers all turned to the same mechanism to express the emotion of the day.

5.4 Opposition-creation and ideology

This book has proposed that there is a phenomenon in many text-types and genres that I have chosen to call constructed opposition (or unconventional opposites) and which seems to behave textually in fairly similar ways in a wide range of contexts, though with different ideational and probably also different ideological effects.

In this final chapter I have been asking whether some of the cognitive theories that have developed in recent years may have explanatory power in dealing with what at first looks like a challenge to the division between competence and performance or langue and parole, since the same kinds of semantic relation that we would allocate to these codified aspects of language are seen to be being set up within texts and interpreted in similar ways to the conventional opposites.

The previous sections have suggested that we may have some kind of image-schema that preconceptually lays down the idea of oppositeness in general and that we may store particular learned examples of this relation in long-term memory. The cognitive explanation for textually constructed and unconventional opposites is that they are processed during reading by drawing on the basic image-schema, on analogy with the known examples and in the framework of the opposite schema which dictates the 'rules' for opposite-creation. The most extreme examples will have no semantic similarity, except for the one component of meaning upon which the distinction depends.

In attempting to answer the question of how readers respond to a text with constructed opposites I have turned to text world theory to hypothesize that readers are invited to 'furnish' a mental model of the text world that they are reading about and that part of this process involves learning about any differences between the reader's 'actual world' and the opposition-construction of the text world. Although frequently used to explain readers' engagement with fictional texts, and thus fictional worlds, this model of the reading process is potentially useful in conceptualizing the possible effects on readers of non-fiction texts too.

McIntyre (2006) invokes possible worlds theory and deictic shift theory to explicate the shift of the reader's 'realm of possibilities' (Ryan 1991:22) and deictic centre, which shift at the start of reading from the reader's actual world to the actual world of the narrator and the deictic centre of the text. Because reading non-fiction is not normally seen as presenting a challenge to the reader's understanding because it relates to the actual world, the question of whether the same process is at work is not addressed specifically in the literature on possible worlds and deictic shifting and it is left to the occasional example to make the point that the same processes are likely to be at work here, only (it is implied) in not such an interesting way.

I would like to use the final part of this book to explore the possibility that far from being less interesting, the processes by which we read non-fiction is not only fascinating, but also vital to explain the influence that constructed oppositions may have on readers' perceptions. Although the extremes of Orwellian brain-washing may have been discredited in the post-*1984* world, there is as I write a new paranoia breaking out about the processes by which young men and women throughout the world are persuaded that killing themselves and others in suicide bombings is the right and virtuous thing to do. At the same time, a successful ballet dancer working in a highly multi-cultural field has joined the right-wing and racist British National Party and the religious right is on the rise in the United States. These people will all have been persuaded of the correctness of their world-view by someone using language, whether in a mosque, a church, a magazine or a private conversation. Somewhere in that language is the key to changes of world-view and, I would argue, the text world that is presented by such language and the deictic centre that the hearer/reader is invited to take up must be key to understanding this process.

Ryan (1991) puts forward a 'principle of minimal departure' as part of her explanation of how readers interpret the possible worlds of texts. She suggests that readers will expect a world described by a text to resemble the actual world in all respects unless they are explicitly told differently. Ryan and others working in this field (Semino 1997; Werth 1999; McIntyre 2006) often deal mainly with fictional texts and try to explain how readers engage with the rather different worlds they encounter when they are reading science fiction or a historical novel and what differences this makes to their reading processes. Where other commentators do look at non-fiction texts, the specific context of reading of such a text is not always considered.

In the case of non-literary texts, I would argue, the same basic process is likely to obtain, with the Principle of Minimal Departure creating the assumption that the text world will be as similar to the reader's actual world as possible unless something explicitly challenges this assumption. If we read a news article about the invasion of Iraq in the year 2007, and the Principle of Minimal Departure applies, then we have a potential cognitive explanation for some of the ideological effects of the mass media. Not only are we aware of reading something that purports to be true, we are also inevitably going to read the text 'as though' it were true, because we even do that when we know it isn't (i.e. in reading fiction). This phenomenon, called by Coleridge (1817:314) 'that *willing suspension of disbelief* for the moment, which constitutes poetic faith' will predispose the reader, at least for the duration of the reading, to accept any meanings that do not seem to be clearly at odds with the actual world we live in. Thus, the construction of unconventional opposites, which are at least interpretable on analogy with oppositions that we are familiar with, will not necessarily be foregrounded as belonging to a possible world phenomenon, rather than being a characteristic of the reader's actual world. Even where we are made aware, by some foregrounding feature, that the created opposite is not to be assumed, the experience of reading itself would require a suspension of the actual world for the duration. This means that, like reading science fiction or historical novels, reading a non-fiction text with clear possible world features may still require us to suspend our disbelief for the duration of reading.

To return to the hypothetical news article about the invasion of Iraq, we might find that it seems to be setting up an opposition, for example, between *Islam* and *The West*. The reader is invited to conclude that the world is so divided because it is one of the structuring devices of the text world and is necessary to understanding the whole text. While sub-disciplines of linguistics such as Critical Discourse Analysis have long asserted the truth of a Whorfian-style effect of culturally dominant texts, they have also been criticized for making too much of this in the absence of hard evidence of the process by which such hegemonic power is wielded and the objection that readers are not so vulnerable to ideological manipulation as the statements may suggest. However, the use of cognitive theories such as possible worlds or text world theory as an 'explanatory' device could help us to understand the mechanisms by which some such ideological influence may indeed operate. The text world set up by a newspaper article on Iraq would of course be purporting to reflect the actual world as seen by the journalist and editor resulting in the reader possibly having no clear reason to resist the notion that the world is indeed so divided.

The experience of reading (or hearing/seeing) fiction may not have a long-term effect on our world-view as readers. Though we immerse ourselves in the world of polite society in the late 18th century to read a Jane Austen novel, and in the world of aliens and space travel to watch *Star Wars* movies, we are likely to revert to our own world-view pretty soon after the end of the experience, though a truly involving novel or film may sometimes leave us with the after-effects of having inhabited a different world for a few minutes or hours. This deictic shifting back from the deictic centre of the fiction to our own, and from a world where different laws – and different oppositions – apply, is one that is assumed in these theories and not explored in any detail.

However, in the case of non-fiction, this shift *out* of a text is vitally important. If we are presented time and again in our daily newspapers, for example, with a world in which Russia (during the Cold War) or Islam (in the early 21st century) are the 'opposite' of all that is good, right and us (i.e. bad, wrong and them) and if in entering that world for a few minutes on the train each morning we assimilate that text world as our own, as we are bound to do to be a successful reader of the texts, then it is a matter of conjecture, or as I hope in future, testing, that this world-view may become our own. First, it is presented as 'true', secondly we have to enter the world to read, thirdly it is so close in almost all respects to the actual world we inhabit that the shifting into and out of the text world may be or become over time an unconscious shift and smoother than the suspension that we sense when we open a novel for the first time.

The thesis in the whole of this book is that texts can – and many do – create new or unusual opposites for their own local purposes, and these opposites are more or less easily interpreted by readers. If we take a deictic view of these constructed opposites, there is often a clear preference for one or other of the terms of the opposition. Take the following example, from the United States' Space Command's Vision 2020, a document outlining the future of likely combat including the use of space:

> The precision and lethality of future weapons will lead to increased massing of effects rather than massing of forces.

This sentence presupposes the increased precision and lethality of the weapons of the future, and the outcome of this development is presented using parallel structures (verbal noun *massing* plus prepositional phrase *of* . . .) to create an opposition between *effects* and *forces*. The new weapons, then, are so powerful and accurate that they can have a greater effect than old-style troop movement. There is a temptation to use the same elegance of parallel structures to perform an intervention in this sentence, putting the people back into the text. Thus:

> The precision and lethality of future weapons will lead to increased killing of enemies rather than killing of friends.

When we read this sentence, or the original, out of context, it is relatively easy to hang onto our own personal liberal values and feel shocked at such a hard-faced statement. However, in its context of a text arguing for increased resources for the US military and particularly for weapons in space, this sentence can only be read from within, and the deictic centre of the reader obliges him/her to understand, if not consciously agree with, the terms of the argument being put forward. If you are indeed going to engage in wars with 'rogue states' and 'non-state actors', it must also be preferable to kill more enemies than allies. Note that Jones (2002) and Davies (2008) both mention the tendency for some of the more common triggers, particularly negation but also what Davies calls *replacive opposition*, to produce a preference for one or other member of the pair. Here, we have a replacive triggered by *rather than*, which together with the evaluative connotations of *enemies* (negative) and *friends* (positive) lead the reader to conclude that the first option is the preferred one.

This trick of rhetoric, whereby the reader is persuaded to adopt the desired viewpoint by presenting it as a complementary opposite to something clearly undesirable (in this case a large number of ground troops) is as old, at least, as Aristotle whose contribution to the debate about opposites went beyond the development of logic, as Lloyd (1966) points out:

> And if Aristotle explicitly investigated the logic of the use of opposites, he also threw some light on the psychology of certain argumentative devices based on opposites which are similar to those we find used in earlier Greek writers. Indeed we saw that in the context of 'rhetorical' arguments he expressly recommends the juxtaposition of contraries as a means of securing admissions from an unwary opponent. We may conclude, then, that important though the analysis of the different modes of opposition was from the point of view of formal logic, the effect of the advances we have considered was not so much to preclude the use of certain types of argument based on opposites, as to enable a dividing line to be drawn between those that have a claim to be demonstrative, and those that are at best persuasive, or at worst frankly misleading. (Lloyd 1966:170–1)

5.5 Opposition and universality

In this book, I have explored a phenomenon, created opposition, which appears to occur in texts of all sorts, though I have yet to discover the extent of its use in conversational interaction. I have demonstrated the range of contexts or triggers that I and others have found so far for opposition, whether conventional or not, and I have tried to place these findings in the context of the data examined by looking at their local textual effects, depending on topic and content and/or text-type and context as appropriate. Finally, I have considered what we might learn from cognitive theories about the processing of unconventional opposites, and the extent to which these might help explain the potential influence of ideologically loaded texts on their readers.

In the process, I have proposed an opposition image-schema which if accepted, would be one of the fundamental building-blocks of human existence and understanding. If so, it presumably arises from some basic bodily experience such as that proposed by Lacan as the mirror stage of development when children first recognize themselves as separate entities from others. This proposal, which is of course not amenable to direct observation or testing, would, if established, indicate that opposition is likely to be a universal feature of human cognition and thus of human language.

The only investigation that I have encountered which may begin to address this question is one which uses linguistic data to postulate universals of human cognition, and is the work of Wierzbicka (1992) and others, who have attempted to produce a set of cognitive semantic primitives from their investigations of different languages' resources. Wierzbicka's list of 'semantic primitives' (Wierzbicka 1972) initially included only fourteen candidates for the fundamental building-blocks of human meaning as follows:

I, you, someone, something, this, want, don't want, think, imagine, feel, part, world, say, become.

Later work by Wierzbicka and others (see Wierzbicka 1992:10 for details) on a range of languages leads her to the conclusion that the list should also include *know, where* and *good* and that other candidates for inclusion in a list of universal semantic fundamentals may also be *when, can, like, the same, kind of, after, do, happen, bad, all, because, if,* and *two*. She also says that some of her original candidates, *part, become, imagine* and *world* are problematic, presumably because she has found languages in which they seem to play no part.

What is interesting for my purposes here is that in Wierzbicka's list there is only one clear candidate for a conventional opposition and at the early stage, only the positive term in that opposition: *good,* was included, though *bad* was later considered possible too.[4] It may be, therefore, that the archetypal opposite in human cognition turns out to be *good-bad.* However, it is not clear, if this is so, how or whether this distinction corresponds to the postulated image-schema of *I-other,* unless of course the *I* is identified as good and *other* is bad, which may well correspond to some cultural theories of self/other.

It will take further work to establish whether there is indeed a universal concept of opposition in the world's languages and to what extent this predisposes readers/hearers to interpret juxtaposed linguistic items (whether words, phrases or larger extracts) as opposites. There is also more to do in discovering the process by which created opposites are interpreted, and whether there are intermediate, culturally determined, but nevertheless basic opposites which are recognizable out of context, and are the reference point for readers trying to interpret textually created opposite-constructions. Note that Davies (2008:41) explains the interpretation of created opposites in terms of what he calls 'superordinates'. These are very similar to the set of basic conventional opposites that I am postulating here. One way of testing these to some degree is to ask whether all the examples of created opposites in the data of whatever kind are easily translatable into a more conventional form. This can be done by the researcher, but would benefit from informant testing in the future, to establish whether there is any consensus about such translations.

Notes

Chapter 1

1 Since the initial work for this book was completed, my student Matt Davies has completed a PhD in this field, and I would like to acknowledge his influence on much of what follows. I hope that his comprehensive work on the formal and ideological aspects of opposite-construction in texts will be published in due course, but in the meantime, readers may consult the thesis (Davies 2008).

2 The archive of Conservative Party documents in the Bodleian library lists two versions, one with 'Indian' and one with 'African' in brackets following the slogan. This presumably refers to the apparent country of origin of the man in the photo, though I only remember seeing the 'African' one. The listing is at: http://www.bodley.ox.ac.uk/dept/scwmss/wmss/online/modern/cpa/library/posters.html#posters.AD

3 The lowest level 'test' on opposites for children on the 'Toon University' website included night/day, up/down, stop/go, short/tall, win/lose. In other words, examples of different categories of opposite are taught to children as equal members of one larger category.

4 This is postulated on analogy with the idea of 'folk etymology' whereby speakers believe that certain words are related (or unrelated) historically when the opposite is the case. 'Folk semantics' can include notions of what words mean (such as the difference between *walk* and *run* being a question of speed) when it is in fact a question of whether there is always one foot in contact with the ground. In the case mentioned here, the notion that opposition is a question of complete difference is under scrutiny.

5 This is so far only attested anecdotally, when groups of students or academics are sometimes asked to provide opposites for a set of words, including for example *dog* and *cabbage,* to see at what point they cease to suggest possible opposites.

6 This summary of how children learn about opposites is hypothetical and would benefit from some serious experimental work to establish whether it reflects the cognitive development of children closely.

Chapter 2

1 This extract was found on the following website on 13th April 2009. http://www.huffingtonpost.com/2008/11/04/obama-victory-speech_n_141194.html. There are many other places on the internet that the text of this speech may be found.

2 Davies (2008:19) discusses the significance of phrasal and clausal opposition-creation and notes that although the corpus approaches of Mettinger and Jones are rigorous and helpful to this study, they go no further than categorizing the contexts of *pre-selected* antonymical pairs and hence miss an opportunity to use the syntactic frames to discover *other* kinds of oppositional pairings, including those which consist of whole phrases and clauses.

Chapter 3

1 I would like to thank Chris Paston, Research Assistant at the time, who was the primary analyst for this piece of work.

2 Though a corpus-based and possibly quantitative study will be the next step in taking the analysis of unconventional opposition further. Note, however, that the triggers will not provide a good basis for quantifying, as they co-occur almost as often as they occur separately.

3 *The Cement Garden, The Comfort of Strangers, In Between the Sheets* and *First Love, Last Rites* were examined.

4 Works consulted were *The Stand, Desperation* and *Dreamcatcher*.

5 Readers unfamiliar with the stylistic notion of 'foregrounding' may wish to consult Leech (2008) for more information.

6 There is no space here to investigate the interface between free indirect style and the creation of opposites, though such an investigation could contribute to our understanding of the use of constructed opposition in dialogue versus narration. Readers unfamiliar with the concept of free indirect style may wish to consult Short (ref) as a starting point.

7 See, for example, Kipling's *Kim,* whose eponymous protagonist is just such a figure, though the complex political loyalties of Kipling and other similar writers such as Rider Haggard mean that the hybrid figure may operate in a number of ways, both in support of and to critique the colonial ideology. I am grateful to Merrick Burrow for these observations (personal communication).

8 The two being *Cause of Death* and *Unnatural Exposure.*

9 Note that one of the examples in Chapter Two, from Medbh McGuckian, creates this very opposition: *with the rage/Of one moment, the contentment of the next.*

10 These are *The Client* (1993), *Testament* (1999) and *Brethren* (2000), all London: Arrow Books.

Chapter 4

1 Although I am not using Text World Theory (Werth 1999) here, the textual construction of opposition may be the kind of 'world-building element' that practitioners in this field could add to their set of analytical tools.

2 It may be indicative that two years running (2005 and 2006), students at Huddersfield University who have chosen to study a module called 'Language and Power' have been generally unaware of the meanings of *left* and *right* in political terms.

3 Davies (unpublished PhD thesis) has argued that we can use blending theory to understand the processing of these constructed opposites in terms of more abstract and conventional oppositions.

4 This assertion (that *democracy* is perceived as an absolute good) is one that needs testing, and would benefit from a corpus approach to work out whether recent usage of the word has been consistently positive in its semantic prosody, and whether this is a recent development or one that has a long history.

Chapter 5

1 Note that Murphy uses the term *antonymy* as her general label for all things opposite. This is not the usual practice in lexical semantics where *antonymy* is often restricted to use in referring to gradable opposition.

2 Lacan's work can be seen in recent translation in Fink (Tr) 2006 and in Lacan 1953.

3 Possible Worlds Theory was a response, arising out of philosophy and logic, to some of the problems produced by truth conditional semantics, where the impossibility of assessing the truth values of fictional worlds made it difficult to develop semantic theory beyond the mundane. I am not going to discuss how it differs from Text World Theory here, but for readers interested in this distinction, see Semino (1997) and Gavins (2007: 11–12, 28–29).

4 Note that in Plato's notion of 'eternal forms', the antonyms like good-bad were problematic as he did not want to include evaluatively negative terms like *bad, ugly* etc. as he was attempting to define the concept of beauty (see Cooper and Hutchinson 1997 for more information).

Bibliography

Ackrill, J. (trans. 1975) Aristotle *Categories and De Interpretatione* (Clarendon Aristotle Series). Oxford: Clarendon Press.

Atkinson, M. (1984) *Our Masters' Voices: Language and Body Language of Politics*. London: Routledge.

Brewer, W. and Brandon Stone, J. (1975) 'Acquisition of spatial antonym pairs.' *Journal of Experimental Psychology* 19: 299–307.

Coleridge, S. T. (1817) *Biographia Literaria* in *Samuel Taylor Coleridge,* ed. by H. J. Jackson, *Samuel Taylor Coleridge*. Oxford: Oxford University Press, The Oxford Authors, 1985.

Cook, G. (1994) *Discourse and Literature: The Interplay of Form and Mind*. Oxford: Oxford University Press.

Cornwell, P. (2001) *The Final Precinct*. New York: Time Warner.

Cruse, D. (1986) *Lexical Semantics*. Cambridge: Cambridge University Press.

Cruse, D. A. (2004) 2nd ed. *Meaning in Language: An Introduction to Semantics and Pragmatics*. Oxford: Oxford University Press.

Culler, J. (1975) *Structuralist Poetics*. London: Routledge and Kegan Paul.

Davern, M. and Cummins, R. (2006) 'Is life dissatisfaction the opposite of life satisfaction?' *Australian Journal of Psychology* 58(1): 1–7.

Davies, M. 'The attraction of opposites: the ideological function of conventional and created oppositions in the construction of in-groups and out-groups in news texts'. Unpublished PhD thesis. University of Huddersfield, 2008.

Derrida, J. (1967) *Writing and Difference*. (trans. Bass, A. 1978. Chicago: University of Chicago Press.)

Duffy, C. (1994) *Selected Poems*. Harmondsworth: Penguin.

Emmott, C. (1997) *Narrative Comprehension. A Discourse Perspective*. Cambridge: Cambridge University Press.

Estes, Z. and Ward, T. (2002) 'The emergence of novel attributes in concept modification.' *Creativity Research Journal* 14(2): 149–56.

Eysenck, M. W. and Keane, M. T. (1990) *Cognitive Psychology: A Student's Handbook*. Hove and London: Lawrence Erlbaum Associates.

Fauconnier, G. (1995) 2nd ed. *Mental Spaces*. Cambridge, Mass: MIT Press.

Faulks, S. (2006) *Human Traces*. London: Vintage.

Feder, E., Rawlinson, M. and Zakin, E. (1997) (eds) *Derrida and Feminism: Recasting the Question of Woman*. London: Routledge.

Fillmore, C. (1982) 'Frame semantics.' In The Linguistic Society of Korea (ed.) *Linguistics in the Morning Calm*. Seoul: Hannshin Publishing Co., 111–38.

— (1985) 'Frames and the semantics of understanding.' *Quaderni di Semantica* VI 2: 222–53.

Gibbs, R. (1994) *The Poetics of Mind: Figurative Thought, Language, and Understanding*. New York: Cambridge University Press.

Gibbs, R. and Steen, G. (eds) (1999) *Metaphor in Cognitive Linguistics*. Amsterdam: John Benjamins.

Grice, P. (1975) *Logic and Conversation*. In Cole, P. and Morgan, J. (eds) Syntax and semantics, vol. 3. New York: Academic Press.

Grisham, J. (2000) *The Brethren*. New York: Island Books.

Hardy, T. (1891) *On the Western Circuit*. English Illustrated Magazine. December 1891, 275–6.

Hegel, G. W. F. (1874) *The Logic of Hegel: Translated from the Encyclopaedia of the Philosophical Sciences with Prolegomena/by William Wallace*. Oxford: Clarendon Press.

Heidenheimer, P. (1978) 'Logical relations in the semantic processing of children between six and ten: emergence of antonym and synonym categorization.' *Child Development* 49:1243–6.

Jeffries, L. (1993) *The Language of Twentieth Century Poetry*. Basingstoke: Macmillan.

— (1994) 'Language in common: apposition in contemporary poetry by women.' In *Feminist Linguistics in Literary Criticism,* Katie Wales (ed.) Boydell and Brewer 21–50.

— (1998) *Meaning in English*. Basingstoke: Macmillan.

— (2000) 'Don't throw out the baby with the bathwater: in defence of theoretical eclecticism in Stylistics.' Pala Occasional Papers 12.

— (2001) 'Schema affirmation and White Asparagus: cultural multilingualism among readers of texts.' *Language and Literature* 10(4): 325–43.

— (2003) 'Not a drop to drink: emerging meanings in local newspaper reporting of the 1995 water crisis in Yorkshire.' *Text* 23(4): 513–38.

— (2007a) *Constructing the Female Body*. Basingstoke: Palgrave.

— (2007b) 'Journalistic constructions of Blair's "apology" for the intelligence leading to the Iraq war.' Johnson, S. and Ensslin, A. (eds) (2007) *Language in the Media: Representations, Identities, Ideologies*. London: Continuum Press. Pages 48–69.

Johnson, M. (1987). *The Body in the Mind: The Bodily Basis of Meaning, Imagination, and Reason.* Chicago: University of Chicago Press.

Jones, S. (2002) *Antonymy: A Corpus-based Perspective.* London and New York: Routledge.

Jones, S. and Murphy, L. (2003) Antonymy in childhood: a corpus-based approach to acquisition. In Archer, D., P. Rayson, A. Wilson and T. McEnery (eds) 2003. UCREL technical paper number 16. UCREL, Lancaster University. Proceedings of the Corpus Linguistics 2003 conference. 372.

Jones, Steven, and M. Lynne Murphy (2005) Using corpora to investigate antonym acquisition. *International Journal of Corpus Linguistics.* 10:3, 401–22.

Lacan, J. *Écrits: The First Complete Edition in English,* transl. by Bruce Fink, New York: W. W. Norton & Co. 2006.

— Some reflections on the Ego, *International Journal of Psychoanalysis,* 1953. French edition *Le Coq Héron,* Paris, 1980.

Lakoff, G. (1982) *Categories and Cognitive Models.* Trier: Linguistic Agency University of Trier.

— (1993) 'The contemporary theory of metaphor.' In A. Ortony (ed.), *Metaphor and Thought* (2nd ed., pp. 202–51). New York: Cambridge University Press.

Lakoff, G. and Johnson, M. (1980) *Metaphors We Live By.* Chicago: University of Chicago Press.

Larkin, P. (1945) *The North Ship.* London: Faber and Faber.

Levi-Strauss, C. (1963) *Structural Anthropology.* Basic Books. Translated by Jakobson, C. and Schoepfe, B. New York: Basic Books.

Lloyd, G. E. R. (1966) *Polarity and Analogy. Two Types of Argumentation in Early Greek Thought.* Cambridge: Cambridge University Press.

Lyons, J. (1977) *Semantics I.* Cambridge: Cambridge University Press.

McGuckian (1994) *Venus and the Rain.* Loughcrew: The Gallery Press.

McIntyre, D. (2006) *Point of View in Plays.* Amsterdam: John Benjamins.

Mettinger, A. (1994) *Aspects of Semantic Opposition in English.* Oxford: Oxford University Press.

Morrison, T. (1982) *Sula.* London: Triad Grafton.

Murphy, G. and Andrew, J. (1993) 'The conceptual basis of antonymy and synonymy in adjectives.' *Journal of Memory and Language* 32: 301–19.

Murphy, M. L. (2003) *Semantic Relations and the Lexicon.* Cambridge: Cambridge University Press.

Nida, E. A. (1975) *Componential Analysis of Meaning.* Paris: Mouton.

Parsons, T. (1997) 'The Traditional Square of Opposition' *Acta Analytica,* 18: 23–49.

— (2001) *One for My Baby.* London: Bloomsbury Publishing.

Peirce, C. S. (1931–35) *Collected Papers,* vols 1–6, Cambridge: Harvard University Press.

— (1958) *Collected Papers,* vols 7–8, Cambridge: Harvard University Press.

Phillips, C. (2004) 'Necessary journeys.' *The Guardian* Saturday, 11th October 2004. Accessed online on 24th January 2007 at: http:// books.guardian.co.uk/review/story/0,,1370289,00.html#article_ continue

Plato (1997) *Complete Works,* ed. by John M. Cooper and D. S Hutchinson. Indianapolis: Hackett.

Rosch, E. (1973) 'Natural categories.' *Cognitive Psychology.* 4:328–50.

— (1978) 'Principles of categorisation.' In Rosch, E. and Lloyd, B. (eds) *Cognition and Categorisation.* Hillsdale, New Jersey: Lawrence Erlbaum Associates.

Russell, B. (1912) *The Problems of Philosophy, With a New Introduction by John Perry.* New York: Oxford University Press, 1997 edition.

Ryan, M. L. (1991) *Possible Worlds, Artificial Intelligence and Narrative Theory.* Bloomington and Indianapolis: Indiana University Press.

Santibáñez, F. (2002) 'The object image-schema and other dependent schemas.' *Atlantis Journal* 24(2) 183–201.

Schank, R. C. and Abelson, R. (1977) *Scripts, Plans, Goals and Understanding.* Hillsdale, New Jersey: Lawrence Erlbaum Associates.

Scott, W., Kline, J., Faguy-Coté, E. and Peterson, C. (1980) 'Centrality of cognitive attributes. *Journal of Research in Personality,* 14 (1): 12–26.

Semino, E. (1995) 'Schema theory and the analysis of text worlds in poetry.' *Language and Literature* 4(2): 79–108.

— (1997) *Language and World Creation in Poems and Other Texts.* Harlow: Addison Wesley Longman.

Shen, Y. (2002) 'Cognitive constraints on verbal creativity. The use of figurative language in poetic discourse.' In Semino and Culpeper (eds) *Cognitive Stylistics. Language and Cognition in Text Analysis.* Amsterdam: John Benjamins 212–30.

Simpson, P. (1993) *Language, Ideology and Point of View.* London: Routledge.

Steen, G. (2002) 'Towards a procedure for metaphor identification.' *Language and Literature* 11(1), 17–33.

Stockwell, P. (2002) *Cognitive Poetics: An Introduction.* London: Routledge.

Werth, P. (1999) *Text Worlds: Representing Conceptual Space in Discourse.* Harlow: Pearson Education.

Wierzbicka, A. (1992) *Semantics, Culture, and Cognition: Universal Human Concepts in Culture-Specific Configurations.* Oxford: Oxford University Press.

Index